122 927

£9.95

KEY
WOMEN
WRITERS
EDITOR: SUE ROE

ELIZABETH GASKELL

KU-545-281

B.C.H.E. — LIBRARY

00103824

KEY
WOMEN
WRITERS
EDITOR: SUE ROE

ELIZABETH GASKELL

PATSY STONEMAN

Lecturer in English
University of Hull

THE HARVESTER PRESS

First published in Great Britain in 1987 by
THE HARVESTER PRESS LIMITED
Publisher: John Spiers
16 Ship Street, Brighton, Sussex

© Patsy Stoneman, 1987

British Library Cataloguing in Publication Data

Stoneman, Patsy
  Elizabeth Gaskell.—(Key women writers)
  1. Gaskell, Elizabeth—Criticism and
  interpretation
  I. Title II. Series
  823'.8   PR4711

  ISBN 0-7108-0577-2
  ISBN 0-7108-0582-9 Pbk

BATH COLLEGE
OF
HIGHER EDUCATION
NEWTON PARK
LIBRARY
C-E.
CLASS
No. 823.8 GAS S
ACC
No. 122 927

Typeset in 11/13pt. Andover by Gilbert Composing Services
Printed in Great Britain by Mackays of Chatham Ltd, Kent

All rights reserved

THE HARVESTER PRESS PUBLISHING GROUP
The Harvester Group comprises Harvester Press Ltd (chiefly
publishing literature, fiction, philosophy, psychology, and
science and trade books); Harvester Press Microform Publications Ltd (publishing in microform previously unpublished
archives, scarce printed sources, and indexes to these
collections) and Wheatsheaf Books Ltd (chiefly publishing in
economics, international politics, sociology, women's studies
and related social sciences).

This book is dedicated to the person who
made me feel able to write it

Titles in the Key Women Writers Series

Key Women Writers
Series Editor: Sue Roe

The *Key Women Writers* series has developed in a spirit of challenge, exploration and interrogation. Looking again at the work of women writers with established places in the mainstream of the literary tradition, the series asks, in what ways can such writers be regarded as feminist? Does their status as canonical writers ignore the notion that there are ways of writing and thinking which are specific to women? Or is it the case that such writers have integrated within their writing a feminist perspective which so subtly maintains its place that these are writers who have, hitherto, been largely misread?

In answering these questions, each volume in the series is attentive to aspects of composition such as style and voice, as well as to the ideas and issues to emerge out of women's writing practice. For while recent developments in literary and feminist theory have played a significant part in the creation of the series, feminist theory represents no specific methodology, but rather an opportunity to broaden our range of responses to the issues of history, psychology and gender which have always engaged women writers. A new and creative dynamics between a woman critic and her female subject has been made possible by recent developments in feminist theory, and the series seeks to reflect the important critical insights which have emerged out of this new, essentially feminist, style of engagement.

It is not always the case that literary theory can be directly transposed from its sources in other disciplines to the practice of reading writing by women. The series investigates the possibility that a distinction may need to be made between feminist politics and the literary criticism of women's writing which has not, up to now, been sufficiently emphasized. Feminist reading, as well as feminist writing, still needs to be constantly interpreted and re-interpreted. The complexity and range of choices implicit in this procedure are represented throughout the series. As works of criticism, all the volumes in the series represent wide-ranging and creative styles of discourse, seeking at all times to express the particular resonances and perspectives of individual women writers.

Sue Roe

Contents

x

Preface

One aim of the *Key Women Writers* series is to examine whether women writers have been accepted into the canon of 'English Literature' at the expense of their being misread as women. Few of the women dealt with can have been misread as systematically as 'Mrs Gaskell'. Seen either as a 'lady novelist', author of *Cranford*, or as a 'social-problem novelist', author of *Mary Barton*, Elizabeth Gaskell has never been read in a way which makes sense of her whole output. I shall argue that a feminist approach focusing on the interaction of class and gender can provide such a reading. I am grateful to The Harvester Press for making it possible for me to develop this argument, and to Sue Roe in particular for her prompt, friendly and generous attention.

Several generations of 'Women in Literature' students at Hull have helped clarify the ideas that went into writing this book, and I also appreciate conversations with John Chapple, Chris Devonshire, Shirley Foster, Angela Leighton and Pauline Thomas. Sue Hamilton's application of speech-act theory to Elizabeth Gaskell's work confirms conclusions which I reached by another route, and I am grateful for our many discussions. Marion Shaw has read the whole manuscript and has been an unfailing source of support and good sense. Like everyone who works on Elizabeth Gaskell, I am indebted to John Chapple and Arthur Pollard for their meticulous edition of her letters.

I give thanks to my whole family for cheerfully accepting a recluse in an upstairs room in place of mother, wife and daughter, and especially to my husband Colin, who despite being a man, a natural scientist and a political economist, has lavished upon me that care and attention whose importance should become clear to whoever reads this book to its end.

References and Abbreviations

There are no footnotes in this book; sources are indicated in the text by the author's surname in parentheses and the full reference will be found in the Alphabetical List of References at the end of the book. There is also a brief classified selected bibliography.

The only complete edition of Elizabeth Gaskell's work is the Knutsford edition, in eight volumes, edited by A.W. Ward, published by John Murray, London, 1906. Since much of her work is unknown, I have listed titles below. Because it is difficult to distinguish short 'novels', like *Cranford*, from long 'short stories', like *The Moorland Cottage*, I have broken the convention and italicised *all* titles:

Knutsford

Vol. 1: *Mary Barton, Libbie Marsh's Three Eras, The Sexton's Hero, Clopton House*

Vol. 2: *Cranford, Christmas Storms and Sunshine, Lizzie Leigh, The Well of Pen-Morfa, The Moorland Cottage, The Heart of John Middleton, Disappearances, The Old Nurse's Story, Morton Hall, Huguenots, My French Master, The Squire's Story*

Vol. 3: *Ruth, Cumberland Sheep-Shearers, Modern Greek Songs, Company Manners, Bessy's Troubles at Home, Hand and Heart*

Vol. 4: *North and South*

Vol. 5: *My Lady Ludlow, Round the Sofa, An Accursed Race, The Doom of the Griffiths, Half a Lifetime Ago, The Poor Clare, The Half-Brothers, Mr Harrison's Confessions, The Manchester Marriage*

Vol. 6: *Sylvia's Lovers, An Italian Institution*

Vol. 7: *Cousin Phillis, Lois the Witch, The Crooked Branch, Curious if True, Right at Last, The Grey Woman, Six Weeks at Heppenheim, A Dark Night's Work, The Shah's English Gardener, French Life, Crowley Castle, Two Fragments of Ghost Stories*

Vol. 8: *Wives and Daughters*

For convenience, however, I have referred to the Knutsford edition only when no modern edition is available and have used the Penguin edition wherever there is one. Titles of Elizabeth Gaskell's works, letters and other books frequently referred to in the text are abbreviated as below. Note that numbers following (*L*) are *Letter* numbers and not page numbers. Incidental references to Victorian works available in various editions are to chapter or section rather than page.

Elizabeth Gaskell's Works

C   *Cranford/Cousin Phillis*, ed. Peter Keating (Penguin: Harmondsworth, 1976).

CP   *Cousin Phillis and Other Tales*, ed. Angus Easson, The World's Classics (Oxford University Press: Oxford and New York, 1981).

K1–8 *The Works of Mrs Gaskell*, [The Knutsford edition] 8 vols., ed. A.W. Ward (John Murray: London, 1906).

L   *The Letters of Mrs Gaskell*, ed. J.A.V. Chapple and Arthur Pollard (Manchester University Press: Manchester, 1966). [Note: numbers refer to Letter no. and not page.]

LCB *The Life of Charlotte Brontë*, ed. Alan Shelston
     (Penguin: Harmondsworth, 1975).
MB   *Mary Barton*, ed. Stephen Gill (Penguin:
     Harmondsworth, 1970).
MD   *My Diary: The Early Years of My Daughter Marianne*,
     printed privately by Clement Shorter, London,
     1923.
NS   *North and South*, ed. Martin Dodsworth (Penguin:
     Harmondsworth, 1970).
P   *Elizabeth Gaskell: Four Short Stories*, introduced by
     Anna Walters (Pandora Press, Routledge & Kegan
     Paul: London and Boston, 1983).
R   *Ruth*, introduced by Margaret Lane, Everyman
     edition (Dent: London and New York, 1967).
SL   *Sylvia's Lovers*, ed. Andrew Sanders, The World's
     Classics (Oxford University Press: Oxford and
     New York, 1982).
WD   *Wives and Daughters*, ed. Frank Glover Smith
     (Penguin: Harmondsworth, 1969).

Other Works

NFI [Anon] *The New Female Instructor: or, Young
     Woman's Guide to Domestic Happiness* . . . (Thomas
     Kelly: London, 1824).
W   Mary Wollstonecraft, *A Vindication of the Rights of
     Woman*, Everyman edition (Dent: London, 1929
     [first published 1792]); this edition also contains
     John Stuart Mill's *The Subjection of Women*.

Chapter One

Reading Elizabeth Gaskell: The Story So Far and Some New Suggestions

feminist literary criticism... present[s us] with a radical alteration of our vision, a demand that we see meaning in what has hitherto been empty space. The orthodox plot recedes, and another plot, hitherto submerged in the anonymity of the background, stands out in bold relief like a thumbprint.

(Elaine Showalter 1975: 435)

Some Victorian women's novels, like *Jane Eyre*, have been a major inspiration to the current women's movement (Showalter 1984). Others, like Elizabeth Gaskell's, have been seen as irrelevant or even counter-productive. While Charlotte Brontë has attracted a mass of new feminist readings, Elizabeth Gaskell remains a respectable minor Victorian, colonised up to a point by Marxists, but almost ignored by feminists. This is partly a question of priorities. Although feminist criticism does not depend on congenial subject-matter, since any piece of writing will be imbued with assumptions about

1

gender which it is the business of feminist criticism to make visible, it is understandable that feminist critics should want to begin with texts which clearly address themselves to the problems of 'women's lot'. Elizabeth Gaskell's work, on the contrary, offers neither an explicit *critique* of women's oppression nor fictive situations, like the madwoman in the attic, which invite symbolic interpretation. Her novels appear to present 'women's lot' either as material for social comedy, as in *Cranford*, or as incidental to class struggle, as in *Mary Barton*, and thus hardly to be 'about' women at all.

Readers, however, especially at the academic level, never approach a text without pre-existing ideas about what they will find. Even the simplest notion of what a novel is 'about' is not intuitive but constructed by previous specific interpretations which precondition our response through the diffuse media of education and public opinion. In the rest of this book I shall use various feminist approaches to argue that Elizabeth Gaskell's novels are more 'about' women than has been acknowledged. But before we can make a feminist re-vision of her work, we must understand some previous 'visions'; for what we as readers inherit is not a naked text but a text already clothed with interpretations. I shall begin with Lord David Cecil's vision of 'Mrs Gaskell' as the 'little woman'.

1 *The Story so Far . . .*

i The Writer as Woman

The outstanding fact about Mrs Gaskell is her femininity . . . she was all a woman was expected to be; gentle, domestic, tactful, unintellectual, prone to tears, easily shocked. So far from chafing at the limits imposed on her activities, she accepted them with serene satisfaction. . . .

Reading Elizabeth Gaskell

> Mrs Gaskell was the typical Victorian woman. (Cecil 1934:
> 197–8)

Lord David Cecil's view of Elizabeth Gaskell was the
prevalent one from the late nineteenth century until the
1950s. Assuming, from some inaccurate 'facts' about
her life, that she was 'all a woman was expected to be',
his 'criticism' of her work proceeds by discovering these
qualities in it. Not only she but also her novels are seen
as unintellectual, childlike, cloistered, lavender scented.
Elizabeth Gaskell's reputation, however, was not always
like this. Dale Spender, quoting a thesis by Anna
Walters, shows how this critical stereotype was created
(Spender 1980: 206–11). When *Mary Barton* was pseud-
onymously published in 1848, reviewers found it
'forcible and fair. . . . The truth of it is terrible' (quoted in
Spender 1980: 207). When the author's sex became
known, however, different qualities were identified.
The author's *'diffidence* and *modesty* begin to be cause for
commendation, she is praised for her ability to move her
readers to sympathy.' (p. 207). Elaine Showalter, in 'The
Double Critical Standard', argues that what happened to
Elizabeth Gaskell was part of a general process. 'The
staple of Victorian periodical reviewing' was categorisation according to gender – 'sentiment, refinement, tact'
for women and 'power . . . learning . . . experience' for
men (Showalter 1977: 90). Above all, feeling was felt to
epitomise women's writing, and by the time of *Wives and
Daughters* (1865), Elizabeth Gaskell is seen as:

> able to *move* the reader but not really responsible for what
> she was doing. . . . Her originality, her intellectual
> achievement, her artistic achievement, all are to be veiled
> by 'feminine accomplishment'. Blatant as this strategy has
> been, it has also been successful. By 1929 . . . Stanton
> Whitfield can . . . declare that her writings are 'sweet and

fragrant' . . . a 'nosegay of violets, honeysuckle, lavender, mignonette and sweet briar'. (Spender 1980: 209)

This transformation affected not only the general evaluation of Elizabeth Gaskell's works but also which novels were most valued. As they appeared, *Mary Barton* (1848), *Ruth* (1853) and *North and South* (1854) provoked lengthy debates on the social issues they raised, but as the 'feminine' image of 'Mrs Gaskell' gained hold, these works fell from favour and the more domestic content of *Cranford* (1851) came to be preferred. Cecil positively denounces *Mary Barton* and *North and South:* 'It would have been impossible for her if she had tried, to have found a subject less suited to her talents [than the industrial revolution]. It was neither domestic nor pastoral. (Cecil 1934: 235). Yvonne ffrench, writing in 1949, regards this change in preference as general: 'for at least two decades after her death [in 1865] she was popularly identified as "the author of *Mary Barton*". Three generations later . . . she is established for good as the author of *Cranford*' (quoted in Wright 1965: 88). There is irony, however, in that 'established for good'; the 1950s saw a dramatic reorientation in Gaskell criticism.

ii   The Social-Problem Novelist
In 1954 Kathleen Tillotson published *Novels of the Eighteen-Forties*, dealing at length with *Mary Barton*, together with other 'novels which are essentially "of" the forties' (Tillotson 1956: vii). This historical treatment enabled Tillotson to avoid the gender-stereotyped criticism which had by now assigned to Elizabeth Gaskell 'an impression of dowdiness' (Collins 1953: 60). Tillotson sees *Mary Barton* as 'the outstanding example . . . of a kind of novel which first clearly disengaged itself in the

forties: the novel directly concerned with a social problem, and especially with the "condition-of-England question"' (Tillotson 1956: 202). Although she pleads against 'the old tag of "novel with a purpose"'' (p. 222), the 'old tag' gave *Mary Barton* a new lease of life, and 'Mrs Gaskell' a new image. Within four years both *Mary Barton* and *North and South* had been taken up by the Marxist critics Raymond Williams and Arnold Kettle, and in 'The Industrial Novels' (William 1958) and 'The Early Victorian Social-Problem Novel' (Kettle 1958), Elizabeth Gaskell is bracketed with Disraeli, Kingsley and the Dickens of *Hard Times*, as a novelist who 'provide[s] some of the most vivid descriptions of life in an unsettled industrial society' (Williams 1958: 99).

This view of Elizabeth Gaskell has become the new orthodoxy, substantiated by Cazamian ([1903] 1973), Lucas (1966) and others. It is as the author of *Mary Barton* and *North and South* that Elizabeth Gaskell now appears on university syllabuses, but the new security of her position is bought at the price of a new distortion; she invariably appears as one of the group of 'social-problem novelists', and her non-industrial novels are ignored. If 'the author of *Cranford*' seemed incapable of having written *Mary Barton*, 'the author of *Mary Barton*' seems just as unable to have written *Cranford*. Critics who attempt to respond to the whole body of her work find themselves in a dilemma.

iii Universal Truths

Some, like Allott (1960: 5) and McVeagh (1970a: 6), see Elizabeth Gaskell as a split personality. Others, like Pollard (1965) and Easson (1979), take each novel on its own merits, giving a wealth of information about composition and reception but attempting no unifying thesis. Most full-scale studies since the mid-1960s have, however, attempted to find some principle of unity. Wright (1965) finds it in a social concern which evolves from the problems of industrial cities to the hierarchical county structures of *Wives and Daughters*. Ganz (1969) sees humour as the key and Craik (1975) the provincial settings. Duthie (1980) identifies a number of themes (nature, society, industry, the family, the individual) which run through all the novels. All these writers begin by deploring the industrial/pastoral split in Gaskell criticism (e.g. Wright 1965: 10; Craik 1975: x; Duthie 1980: xi), but none of them is able to produce a formula which heals the breach. As the inadequacy of each 'key' becomes apparent, these critics fall back on the 'universal' values of 'art' (e.g. Ganz 1969: 133; Craik 1975: x). In this process, the 'industrial' novels imperceptibly slide from view and the rural idyll is reinstated as the true Gaskell world (e.g. Wright 1965: 146; Ganz 1969; 166, 223; Duthie 1980: 64–5). Duthie, in the most recent full-length study of Elizabeth Gaskell, settles on *Cranford* as the Gaskell epitome, 'as vital and enduring as the hawthorne in the hedgerows' (Duthie 1980: 37). We have not come far from the Whitfield/Cecil floral school of criticism, which finds *Cranford* 'as fresh as this morning's roses' (Cecil 1934: 241). My inference is that critics who invoke 'universal values' are often merely mouthing the comfortable prejudices of their forefathers (*sic*).

The only full-length study which avoids the slide either towards *Mary Barton* and the social-problem approach or towards *Cranford* and the universal/aesthetic is Coral Lansbury's *Elizabeth Gaskell: The Novel of Social Crisis* (1975). What distinguishes her book is its recognition of the importance of the family in Elizabeth Gaskell's novels. Seeing the family as a basic structure of authority, she is able to make links between novels which

6

are otherwise disparate. A socialist rather than a feminist critic, her treatment of the family as a political force interacting with others nevertheless provides an important basis for a feminist reading.

2 Some Feminist Alternatives

Of all the enormous output of feminist literary criticism during the last fifteen years, none has been concerned to any major extent with Elizabeth Gaskell. Perceived as belonging either to the (masculine) preserve of the 'industrial' novel or the cosy world of the 'lady novelist', her work offered nothing as promising as the Brontë novels or George Eliot. The rest of this chapter, therefore, surveys not finished feminist readings of Elizabeth Gaskell, which do not exist, but general and theoretical approaches which can be adapted to illuminate her work. Elaine Showalter's essays 'Towards a Feminist Poetics' (Jacobus 1979) and 'Feminist Criticism in the Wilderness' (Abel 1982) have been useful in suggesting broad categorisation.

i The Critique of Phallic Criticism
The phrase 'phallic criticism' was invented by Mary Ellmann (1968), and it identifies a widespread assumption by literary critics that writing is properly a masculine activity and that women lack the proper equipment to do it well. Although a critique of phallic criticism tells us nothing new about the text itself, it can tell us why women's writing has been devalued in the past. Cecil, for instance, complains that Elizabeth Gaskell's writing 'lacks . . . virile fire and life' (Cecil 1934: 220). She is 'baffled' by men ('huge, clumsy, hairy creatures', p. 210) and recreates them as 'imperfectly

disguised Victorian women, prudish, timid and demure' (p. 234). The demolition of phallic criticism can be fun, as Ellmann demonstrates, but it raises a serious question which Gilbert and Gubar ask in *The Madwoman in the Attic*: 'if the pen is a metaphorical penis, with what organ can females generate texts?' (Gilbert and Gubar 1979: 7).

Phallic criticism sees women's writing as 'not-male' and therefore inferior – intuitive rather than rational, gentle rather than virile. But what if women are using some other metaphorical organ and writing in ways which do not register on the virilometer? The result would appear, by masculine standards, confused and unfocused, a mixture of blanks and gaps and what seem to be unsuccessful efforts at 'virility'; (she 'makes a creditable effort to overcome her natural deficiencies... but all in vain' (Cecil 1934: 235)). This picture of gaps, confusions and failures is, in fact, what emerges from a survey of Gaskell criticism. One group sees her scoring high on the masculine (social problem) scale, but only in two novels. Another group sees her as properly 'feminine', but with odd forays into 'subjects that did not inspire her' (Cecil 1934: 238). Pervasive through all, there is a kind of irritation with the author for not properly performing what the critic assumes she is trying to do.

Critics of all kinds complain about a lack of 'proportion' and correctness (Spender 1980: 208); 'failure to come to a point' (Collins 1983: 66); 'confusion' of different issues (Wright 1965: 142); inclusion of 'adventitious', 'unnecessary' and 'irrelevant' material (McVeagh, 1970b: 275); and a general lack of focus (Tillotson 1956: 213; Collins 1953: 72; Lucas 1977: 1, 3).

Irritation changes to embarrassment when critics deal with Elizabeth Gaskell's minor works, many of which have subjects – ghosts, bandits, witches, murders, madmen, imprisonment, torture, mutilation – which 'fit' neither her earnest social image nor her cosy feminine one. Many of these stories have been out of print since 1906, and critics tend to dismiss them as 'fancies' (Ward, K I: xliii) or 'melodrama' (Allott 1960: 33).

Catherine Belsey undercuts all this puzzlement and indignation when she writes, 'realism is plausible not because it reflects the world, but because it is constructed out of what is (discursively) familiar. . . . It is intelligible as "realistic" precisely because it reproduces what we already seem to know' (Belsey 1980: 47). Plausibility in literature is thus a matter not of absolute truth but of conventions and maxims. In 'Emphasis Added: Plots and Plausibilities in Women's Fiction', Nancy Miller goes on, 'if no maxim is available to account for a particular piece of behavior, that behavior is read as unmotivated and unconvincing' (Miller 1981: 36). This could explain the lack of focus which critics complain of in Elizabeth Gaskell's work.

If the critics have got it all wrong, however, what can 'make sense' of Elizabeth Gaskell's work? Miller offers an explanation deriving from Freud's theory of repression (p. 41), but we do not need to invoke the unconscious to bring Elizabeth Gaskell's work into focus. Much critical dissatisfaction results simply from applying ready-made labels ('industrial', 'pastoral') or looking for familiar patterns of coherence, and finding that the writing does not match the assumed model. If *Mary Barton* and *North and South* are defined as 'industrial' novels, for instance, it seems logical to deplore their degeneration into 'romance'. But if we see them as exploring the way in which gender-linked ideologies underpin industrial organisation, the disjunction disappears. The labels prejudge the content by separating the 'political' from the 'personal'. Miller concludes:

the attack on female plots and plausibilities assumes that women writers cannot or will not obey the rules of fiction..
. . . [S]ensibility, sensitivity, 'extravagance' . . . are taken to be not merely inferior modalities of production but deviations from some obvious truth. The blind spot here is both political . . . and literary. . . . It does not see that the maxims that pass for the truth of human experience, and the encoding of that experience in literature, are organisations, when they are not fantasies, of the dominant culture. (Miller 1981: 46)

Feminist criticism, by redefining what is 'real', 'rational', 'coherent', allows us to 'see meaning in what has hitherto been empty space' (Showalter 1975: 435). But there is more than one kind of feminist criticism.

ii   The text as Female History
The first kind of feminist criticism which emerged in the 1970s saw fiction as evidence of the lives women have lived. Books by Patricia Beer (1974), Françoise Basch (1974) and Jenni Calder (1976) discuss fictional characters in terms of the real social context, and Basch's book in particular gives a wealth of contemporary documentation about the ideological, legal, social, economic and sexual conditions under which Victorian women lived. This sort of study is essential groundwork for any kind of feminist reading, but it tends to minimise the literary element in writing, assuming that fiction 'reflects' reality in an unproblematic way and ignoring the fact that the process of writing is itself determined by history; literature is produced 'not by magic, but by a real labour of production . . . in determinate conditions' (Macherey 1978: 67–8).

iii   Women as Writers
Another feminist approach, therefore, is to study the

material circumstances in which women wrote: where, when and how they wrote, whether and how much they got paid, published and distributed, which people they knew and what books they read. In 1977 substantial books by Elaine Showalter and Ellen Moers dealt with this area in detail, aiming, in particular, to banish the image of the artist as a lonely genius creating ideas out of her own head.

In one sense literary production is 'material' in that it involves someone sitting in a room pushing a pen across paper. But in another sense books are 'made' not of ink and paper, but of other books. Harold Bloom has theorised the process by which texts are made by selecting, adapting, rejecting or imitating other texts, seeing 'the sequential historical relationship between literary artists [as] the relationship of father and son' (quoted in Gilbert and Gubar 1979: 46). Gilbert and Gubar point out that Bloom's model of 'literary history as the crucial warfare of fathers and sons' (p. 47) defines the woman writer as anomalous, and Showalter's book, *A Literature of Their Own*, is designed to demonstrate that although women have often appeared as isolated figures in a largely male tradition, they are actually supported by a forgotten female tradition which can alter our perspective. Elizabeth Gaskell, who is normally compared with Dickens, Kingsley and Disraeli, shows differently when related to Mary Wollstonecraft, Mary Shelley and Charlotte Brontë. Showalter argues that the rediscovery of minor writers is especially important, since they are 'links in the chain that bound one generation to the next', creating 'the continuities in women's writing' (Showalter 1977: 7).

Remarkably, this work of literary archaeology was begun for Elizabeth Gaskell as early as 1950 by Aina Rubenius, who reconstructs her relationships with a large group of contemporary women writers and feminists, and thus radically revises the traditional view of 'Mrs Gaskell' as a woman wholly sunk in domesticity, who hardly ever looked into a book. I shall discuss these influences in Chapter 2.

The assertion of a female tradition, however, cannot erase the difficulties women writers experience in a predominantly male culture. Where Bloom identifies a characteristic 'anxiety of influence' in writers, Gilbert and Gubar show that women writers suffer a more basic 'anxiety of authorship' (Gilbert and Gubar 1979: 46-9), since for a woman to write at all may be perceived as an act of deviancy. To explore the relationship of women writers to the dominant culture, we must look at language itself as a carrier of social values.

iv   Ideology and the Literary Text

In order to investigate this area, feminist critics have adapted the work of the post-structuralist critics of the 1970s (clearly explained in Catherine Belsey's book *Critical Practice*, 1980). These writers apply to literary criticism the principle of the linguist Ferdinand de Saussure, that an utterance only derives meaning from the language in which it is situated, arguing that the rule applies not only to languages such as French and English but also to value-systems, literary conventions, social codes of conduct, traditional tales of virtue and heroism – systems which Barthes calls 'myths' and Althusser 'ideology'. It is only within a recognised value-system, or ideology, that any utterance, or text, can be meaningful. This poses an inescapable problem to oppressed groups within a culture; they can only be understood by using the language of the dominant group, yet since that language has their inferior status inscribed within it as part of its structure of meanings, any utterance of theirs, whether comformist or defiant, is perceived as confirming their inferiority. As Xavière Gauthier puts it, 'as long as women remain silent, they will be outside the historical process. But, if they begin to speak and write *as men do*, they will enter history subdued and alienated' (in Abel 1982: 21).

For example, because the Victorian ideological 'package' defining the position of women included wife- and motherhood, submission and domesticity, it was difficult for a woman to use the words 'mother' or 'home' without invoking the whole normative structure. Although, as I shall argue later, Elizabeth Gaskell had unusual ideas about motherhood, her unorthodox meanings have been 'subdued', so that Basch, for instance, sees her statements as 'based on a conventional notion of the woman's realm' (Basch 1974: 185). Because language derives its meanings from a closed system of values, the language itself 'subdues' alternative meanings and alienates women writers when they try to express them (see Spender 1980: 54–9).

The 'text as history' approach to women and literature is a relatively blunt instrument, which sees women either as determined by social conditions or as freeing themselves by an act of will. Post-structuralist ideas enable us to see 'the irreducibly complicated relationship women have historically had to the language of the dominant culture' (Miller 1981: 38). A useful tool in analysing this relationship is the sociological concept of dominant and muted groups. Showalter explains that 'women constitute a *muted group*, the boundaries of whose culture and reality overlap, but are not wholly contained by, the *dominant (male) group*' (in Abel 1982: 29; see also Spender 1980: 76–105). According to Showalter, this means that 'women's writing is a "double-voiced discourse" that always

13

embodies the social, literary, and cultural heritages of both the muted and the dominant' (in Abel 1982: 31). A central task for current feminist criticism is thus to disentangle this 'complicated relationship' or, in Showalter's words, 'to plot the precise cultural locus of female literary identity and to describe the forces that intersect an individual woman writer's cultural field' (in Abel 1982: 32). The major forces that intersect Elizabeth Gaskell's cultural field – the ideology of femininity, the language of 'high culture' and the language of Christianity – will be identified in Chapter 2 and form the basis for discussion of the novels throughout the book.

v   Psychoanalytic Criticism

Whereas the critique of ideology takes gender dominance as 'given', psychoanalysis can explain how boys and girls acquire the cultural status of 'men' and 'women' through socialisation within the family. Much feminist criticism uses the terminology of the French psychoanalyst Jacques Lacan (see Eagleton 1983: 151–93; Mitchell and Rose 1982; Belsey 1980), who has defined the acquisition of language, and with it the values of society, as 'entry into the symbolic order'. Lacan highlights the fact that the 'symbolic order' in our society has been determined by men, by describing its historical, mythical and institutional meanings as 'the dead father', 'the paternal metaphor', 'The Name of the Father', 'the letter of the Law'.

These concepts help bring into focus Elizabeth Gaskell's consistent use of fictional plots to dramatise her dissent from the institutions of patriarchy – the law in society and the father in the family. In Chapter 3(4) I shall argue that most of her plots are constructed to highlight the abuse or fallibility of authority; all the melodramatic minor works hinge on its outrageous exercise. Once perceived, this theme appears obsessive in her work, although almost all criticism to date has seen her as an upholder of law and order at all cost. This paradox derives from the fact that the authorial voice in Elizabeth Gaskell's work parades no 'rage and rebellion' but exposes injustice in a tone of mild reason. Psychoanalytic theory accounts for this 'double-voiced discourse', which reveals disturbing meanings only when the focus is altered, by the theory of repression, according to which adult identity is acquired, together with access to language and the values of the symbolic order, at the cost of repressing all unacceptable elements, which form the unconscious. In women, anger, sexuality and the urge to power are generally repressed.

Several feminist critics (Gilbert and Gubar 1979; Jacobus 1979; Miller 1981) have argued that 'female gothic' – sensational plots and monstrous characters – is the unconscious expression of women's repressed urge to power, which, denied social outlets, surfaces in the form of 'unfeminine' fantasies of bloodshed and incarceration. Similarly, repressed sexuality emerges in unconscious patterns of imagery and dream sequences, even in Elizabeth Gaskell's social-problem novels. Although I shall use this idea in discussing Gaskell's murders, ghosts and court-room plots, as well as the sexual psychology of her characters, I shall not, like the advocates of *écriture feminine* (see Marks and de Courtivron 1982), argue that these eccentric features constitute her distinctive strength as a writer. I see them, on the contrary, as symptoms of constraint and disablement, significant but not cause for celebration. The irruptions of the unconscious are most notable in those works, like *Ruth* and *North and South*, whose obviously controversial subject-matter put a strain on the author. Those, like

Cousin Phillis and *Wives and Daughters*, which were perceived by author and readership as non-controversial novels of domestic manners, have few 'extravagant' features and a more confident tone, and yet in them the repressed elements which disturbed the earlier texts – women's urge towards social and sexual autonomy – have become the conscious subject-matter. I see Elizabeth Gaskell's strength as lying less in the inchoate challenges of the unconscious than in a rational challenge to the institutions of the family and the law which takes the form of questioning the polarised roles of 'mother' and 'father'.

vi Marxism, Feminism and the Question of Motherhood

' "Motherhood", no longer a euphemism for the banal and harmless, is about to become a major political issue.' So wrote Mary O'Brien in 1982, in one of a collection of essays entitled *Feminist Theory: A Critique of Ideology* (Keohane, Rosaldo and Gelpi, 1982: 110). Throughout this collection there are signs of a reorientation in feminist thinking about motherhood which began in the mid-1970s; yet in dealing with this issue – one of central importance to Elizabeth Gaskell – I have been helped by no major work of literary theory. Davidson and Broner's *The Lost Tradition* (1980) is too eclectic to be theoretically useful, and I have drawn rather on works combining psychoanalytic and political analysis, written from a materialist feminist perspective. The term 'materialist feminist' is useful, including both explicit Marxists and others whose analysis has a historical, political and economic dimension, but who would not call themselves Marxists (Newton and Rosenfelt 1985: xviii). Since the relationship between Marxism and feminism is problematic, however, my position still needs clarification.

The Marxist critics who resurrected Elizabeth Gaskell in the 1950s took the classic position that all social formations are determined by the relations of production. They were interested in what she had to say about the politics of the work-place, but were oblivious to questions of gender. Twenty years later, the orthodox position on women was still 'that the oppression of women is a consequence of capitalism, and that . . . the liberation of women depends on socialism' (Guettel 1974: jacket blurb). The Marxist feminist Christine Delphy has shown this analysis to be un-Marxist even in orthodox terms, since it ignores the productive labour of women in the home. But she also identifies 'the control of reproduction' as 'the cause and the means for the second great material oppression of women' (Delphy 1977: 19).

For radical feminists, the 'control or reproduction' is not the second but the primary cause of women's oppression, and Adrienne Rich provides a wealth of cultural and personal evidence to support this position in *Of Woman Born: Motherhood as Experience and Institution* (1977). Her 'radical' vision, however, framing motherhood as a question for women alone, is ultimately less able to encompass the enormity of the problem than that of recent materialist feminists who, while accepting the primacy of women's oppression, insist that men as well as women must change. Developing Christine Delphy's position, Mary O'Brien argues that 'the integration of women on equal terms in the productive realm' must be balanced by 'the integration of men into the relations of reproduction and into the active care of the next generation' (in Keohane, Rosaldo and Gelpi 1982: 111). Much more is at issue here than the equitable sharing of labour and rewards. Dorothy Dinnerstein's book *The Rocking of the Cradle and the Ruling of the World* (1976) (known in the United States as *The Mermaid and the Minotaur: Sexual Arrangements and Human Malaise*) gives a powerful sense of the urgency and scope of this programme. She draws on myth, literature, history, psychology and politics to demonstrate that the separation of child-rearing from the public realm is the enabling mechanism for the class war, the rape of natural resources and international aggression. In arguing that this pernicious system can be dismantled only by the involvement of men in primary child-care, she is clear that what is at stake is nothing less than the survival of the planet.

In *The Reproduction of Mothering* (1978) Nancy Chodorow gives an exhaustive and radical psychoanalytic justification for this claim, challenging the inevitability of Freud's Oedipal triangle in which the primary mother-child dyad is interrupted by the culture-bearing father. In Freud's model the mother/woman is inevitably consigned to the pre-human/childish – that which is to be transcended – while 'adulthood' is defined, especially for boys, as what is apart from the mother. Chodorow argues that infants cared for from birth by both men and women who also led full adult lives would experience no discontinuity between the nurturing relationships of childhood and adult life. On the one hand there would be no distinct group of 'care-takers' against which to define 'adulthood'; on the other, memories of infantile intimacy and care would attach to all possible models for adult autonomy. As it is, 'women's mothering is . . . a crucial link between the . . . organization of gender and organization of production' (Chodorow 1978: 219), creating women who must choose between being female and being adult, and men whose resistance to nurture fits them for a cash-nexus economy and a politics of aggression. Only by validating 'maternal' care as a quality appropriate to adult men can we hope to break the aggressive pattern of public and political life, but only women have the motivation to initiate this change. Thus 'women are, in the Marxist sense, the progressive force within these historical developments' (O'Brien, in Keohane, Rosaldo and Gelpi 1982: 111).

As yet there has been little interaction between these political and psychoanalytic studies of motherhood and literary theory. Jean Bethke Elshtain complains that Dinnerstein and Chodorow, for instance, assign 'no specific role to the language-bearing female subject' and ignore 'the potentially creative, unpredictable and surprising possibilities of human speech' (in Keohane. Rosaldo and Gelpi 1982: 143). In this book Dinnerstein and Chodorow provide the broad orientation, but my methods are those of literary criticism, and my focus is on language. I shall try to be alert to the 'double-voiced discourse' and the symptoms of repression endemic in women's writing. But I shall not assume that because Elizabeth Gaskell wrote as a wife and mother, we as feminists must read her texts only for the encoded cry of protest and not for the conscious voice of reason. If accommodation to patriarchal structures always and only signalled acquiescence in one's own oppression, I should not be writing this book in the house where I live, happily, with my mother and father, my husband and my daughters. Elizabeth Gaskell was consciously, as well as unconsciously, aware of gender problems and knew the importance for women of 'speaking out'. Her efforts at social reconstruction were directed precisely towards inducing caring attitudes in men and exposing conventional motherhood as the means of infantilising women. The interest of her texts for us now will inevitably lie at the point where her efforts at problem-solving break down under the pressure of ideology. But if women are to be the 'progressive force' in social change, it is organised thought, not inarticulate resistance, which will achieve it, and if men are to be included in the transformation of motherhood, it is mothers within the family who may well have the most valuable thoughts to offer. In 'Feminist Discourse and Its Discontents' Jean Bethke Elshtain proposes that:

> one moral and political imperative that would unite rather than divide women, that would tap what is already there but go on to redeem and transform it, would be a feminist commitment to a mode of public discourse imbedded within the values and ways of seeing that comprise what Sara Ruddick has called 'maternal thinking'. (in Keohane, Rosaldo and Gelpi 1982: 145)

This book attempts that mode.

Chapter Two

Woman and Writer: Blending the Selves

'Literature cannot be the business of a woman's life, and it ought not to be.'
(Robert Southey to Charlotte Brontë, *LCB*: 173)

1 *The Woman*

Psychologists tell us that artistically creative people are 'emotionally stable, self-confident, self-critical . . . less anxious . . . less dogmatic . . . flexible . . . and able to resist the pressures to conform' (Bardwick 1971: 202–3). Yet historical research reveals the typical Victorian woman as 'a mental and moral cripple, incapable of informed and independent judgement, timid, deferential . . . vacuous . . a slave to conventional opinion, to class prejudice, and to a narrow and bigoted morality. Above all she was a slave to the great shibboleth of propriety' (Trudgill 1976: 66). Clearly a Victorian woman writer was not a 'typical' Victorian woman, and Elizabeth Gaskell's letters (see Chapple 1980) give a delightful sense of her lively and energetic life-style. By contemporary standards she was unconventional; she boasts of eating, walking and blowing her nose, all of which *The New Female Instructor* finds 'indelicate' (*L* 2, 9, 455; *NFI*: 14, 16). In a letter to her sister-in-law she covers 'why the d—' with '(Honi soit qui mal y pense)'. Of a fellow minister's wife, she writes: 'Mrs J.J. Taylor has got an impromptu baby at Blackpool; . . . . Bathing places do so much good. Susan & Mary went to Blackpool last year, but did not derive the same benefit' (*L* 9). Sometimes she is conscious of unorthodoxy, as when she offends the same minister's wife by talking about novels on a Sunday; 'so there I am in a scrape, – well! it can't be helped, I am myself and nobody else, and can't be bound by another's rules' (*L* 32).

Although these letters seem to show Elizabeth Gaskell as an anomaly, 'almost too vivid and aware for her circle' (Chapple 1980: 25), it is misleading to see all Victorian women as 'shackled by a cramping and inflexible domestic ideology' (Stubbs 1979: 9). The 'separate sphere' which could be a prison could also be, within its limits, a field for autonomous action, producing odd contradictions in women's lives. Mrs Ellis, the conduct-book writer, and Mrs Beeton, the writer on domestic economy, made public careers for themselves based on woman's domestic role. Within the household, the servants who are now supposed to have reduced middle-class women to vacuity also called for what we would call personnel management and pastoral care (e.g. *L* 182). 'Good works' involved women in what Chapple calls 'the extraordinary network of Victorian philanthropy' (Chapple 1980: 113) – a largely female network which prompted Fredrika Bremer's proposal for an international women's communications system to bypass formal governments (*The Times*, 28 August 1854). Add to these Elizabeth Gaskell's other duties as a minister's wife, the care of four children and entertainment of friends and relations, and even without writing, her life appears at times one of desperate confusion rather than vacuity:

> Mary has been away since this day 3 weeks; & ever since Thursday week *backwards* the house has been full . . . Mr and Mrs Field . . . Effie . . . a General & Mrs Cotton . . . a Mr MacElroy . . . Mary Holland . . . Emma Shaen . . . & oh dear! Papa is not well with his liver; & you can fancy *how* busy we are, & we can't get Mrs Brett & don't know who to get, & Hearn's keys can't be found –& &. Ellen Tollett comes on Saturday . . . the Shadwells. . . . And it is cutting out Clothing time . . . 1/2 pt 2 to Knutsford to the Concert, respecting which we've had a row with Cousin Mary. . . . Moreover we can't get a *bit* of butter. . . . Tell Hearn *all* her wits are wanted in this desolate butterless, servantless, headless, washerwomanless, company full household. (*L* 478)

This torrent continues for two pages, but there is enjoyment as well as desperation in it; the person Elizabeth Gaskell pities is the one with nothing to do. She sympathises with the feeling of *'purposelessness'* described by the author (Virginia Woolf's 'Aunt Nun') of ' "Passages in the Life of a Daughter at Home" ' (*L* 72), a feeling which, according to Florence Nightingale, 'dooms some minds to incurable infancy, others to silent misery' (Strachey 1978: 404). Elizabeth Gaskell was saved from this doom by her active life as manager of a large household, which, as Mrs Beeton points out, make a woman 'of far more importance in a community than she usually thinks she is' (quoted in Auerbach 1978: 35; cf. Ellis 1839: 73).

Not every Victorian housewife was an Elizabeth Gaskell, however. A number of factors combine to make her exceptional. It is important that her father and husband were Unitarians, whose 'theology was an optimistic affirmation of man as a rational being who could ultimately attain a perfect state in this world' (Lansbury 1975: 11). Unitarian emphasis on reason and individual responsibility mean that no group of people could be regarded as properly under the domination of another. Children, for instance, were educated through games and discussion rather than rote-learning (p. 13) and Unitarian women were 'released from much of the prejudice and oppression enjoined upon other women' (p. 11; cf Fryckstedt 1982: 63–86). Elizabeth Gaskell's father, William Stevenson, was unusual even among Unitarians and gave up his ministry as a protest against payment for preaching (Lansbury, 1975: 11). Afterwards he was a farmer and later a journalist, writing articles on education and political economy (Stevenson 1796, 1824–5) which must have influenced his daughter.

Elizabeth Gaskell's mother, however, died when she was a year old, and she was brought up by her mother's sister, Aunt Lumb. Showalter (1977) and Anderson have argued that the mother's early death is a 'common factor in the lives of . . . nonconforming women' (Anderson 1982: 20), since 'the emergence of highly developed achievement drives in girls' is linked with 'identification with the father' (Showalter 1977: 64). In Elizabeth Gaskell's case, however, Aunt Lumb was not only a richly satisfying mother-substitute but also an independent role-model. Showalter assumes the Oedipal pattern whereby girls reject the 'inferior' mother in favour of the powerful father, normally as love-object, but, for exceptional women, as role-model. Chodorow, however, argues that girls use their fathers as a way of escaping from a mother who is felt to be omnipotent, and that they often also split the mother-image into 'a fearsome . . . maternal image . . . derived from their own feelings of impotence' alongside 'an omnipotent protective mother – thus the witch and the fairy godmother' (Chodorow 1978: 122). Elizabeth Gaskell's father remarried when she was four, and she disliked her stepmother intensely (Gérin 1976: 17), enabling her to project her dislike of maternal control on to the cold-hearted, socially pernicketty stepmother, and to keep 'darling aunt Lumb' (*L* 1), her 'more than mother', as the fairy godmother. Phyllis Chesler argues that 'step-mother' qualities result from mothers' anxiety for daughters' social success; they 'must be harsh in training their daughters to be "feminine" in order that they learn how to serve in order to survive' (Chesler 1974: 19). But Aunt Lumb's household was not patriarchal; there was no man to serve. Homely and decorous, she was still head of the house. Elizabeth Gaskell's unfamiliarity with patriarchy at close quarters may account for her exaggeration, in *The Life of Charlotte Brontë*, of Patrick Brontë's authoritarianism and her astonishment at Charlotte's 'patient docility . . . in her conduct towards her father' (*LCB*: 508, 511). It also explains the apparent inconsistency which puzzles Anderson, that she was able to live in 'conformity to the Victorian female role of wife and mother' and also be 'the real provider and manager of her family' (Anderson 1982: 41). Anderson needs Elizabeth Gaskell to be 'male-identified' to fit her theory, just as Virginia Woolf needs to kill the Angel in the House because the 'difficult arts of family life' (Barrett 1979: 59) are to her the arts of keeping father happy. Neither can see that the arts of household management and personal relationships need not serve *paterfamilias*. Elizabeth Gaskell's stories show them flourishing in all sorts of unorthodox 'families' (see below, Ch. 3), just as she shows that 'the love of parent and child' can 'be established between strangers' (Lansbury 1975: 16).

Chodorow, moreover, argues that 'mothers' who are 'supported by a network of women kin and friends . . . produce daughters with capacities for nurturance and a strong sense of self' (Chodorow 1978: 213). Aunt Lumb was supported by the prolific Holland family; her brother, with two unmarried daughters, and her parents, all lived nearby in Knutsford.

When Elizabeth Gaskell married at the age of 21, she acquired still more relations, notably William Gaskell's sisters, Elizabeth and Anne, and two of his pupils, the Winkworths, whom she 'adopted' as sisters – all became good friends and correspondents. Unitarians, as 'a sect everywhere spoken against' were energetic in maintaining nation-wide links, and Eliza (Tottie) Fox the painter became a close friend, although she lived in London and the Gaskells in Manchester. Other women in this 'network' included Barbara Bodichon, Harriet Martineau, Emily Shaen and Parthenope Nightingale – all active in the cause of women's rights. Holt, the historian of Unitarianism, asserts that 'no religious body except the Quakers has given such wholehearted support . . . to the cause of women's freedom' (Holt 1938: 147).

Other contacts came through writing; the Quaker journalist Mary Howitt published Elizabeth Gaskell's earliest writing and also translated the works of the Swedish feminist Fredrika Bremer, whom Elizabeth Gaskell met in 1851 (L 103–5). Aina Rubenius argues that Gaskell was extensively indebted to Bremer for plots and ideas. Elizabeth Gaskell also knew Mme Mohl, an Irish/French feminist, with whom she stayed several times in Paris, Anna Jameson, who published a mildly feminist work in 1832, and Caroline Norton, author of *English Laws for Women in the Nineteenth Century* (1854). Later she exchanged letters with Elizabeth Barrett Browning and George Eliot, and her friendship with Charlotte Brontë led to *The Life of Charlotte Brontë* (1857). It is indicative of the close sense of shared experience between these women writers, who did not all know one another well, that Elizabeth Gaskell quoted, on the title page of *The Life of Charlotte Brontë*, lines from the newly published *Aurora Leigh*:

> 'How dreary 'tis for women to sit still
> On winter nights by solitary fires
> And hear the nations praising them far off!'

Female friendship was an important counterweight to domesticity, but very few even of the avowed feminists of the period wanted to remove women from the home (cf. Banks and Banks 1964: 48-9; W 70). Many sympathised with Elizabeth Gaskell's dislike of 'speech-making . . . and such noisy obtrusive ways of "doing good"' (L 123). Florence Nightingale, whom she admired to adulation (e.g. L 211), posed a problem for Elizabeth Gaskell because of her lack of human ties; 'she has no friend – and she wants none. . . . She and I had a grand quarrel one day. She is . . . too much for institutions . . . if she had influence enough not a mother should bring up a child herself'. (L 217). It is significant that *'Florence Nightingale* described herself as "brutally indifferent to the rights and wrongs" of her sex' (Holt 1938: 148) and organised her nursing school on hierarchical principles borrowed from the army, creating bonds which Mary Daly sees as typical of male comradeship rather than 'sisterhood' (Daly 1979: 369-70).

Elizabeth Gaskell sees the value of organisations to give support and usefulness to single women but fears that abstract causes may make women 'desert the post

27

where God has placed them' (L 72). All her comments assume that girls and women have natural 'home-duties'; hers is a rosy version of the life which nearly drove Florence Nightingale mad. The contrast between the two women need not, however, be seen in terms of convention versus revolt. Gaskell's domesticity combines with a robust sense of female bonding to contrast with the lone daring of a saint, or the general of an army.

As early as 1838, however, we find Elizabeth Gaskell conscious of tension between home duties and a longing for freedom. In an image which Moers (1978: 245-51) and Kaplan (1976: 35) identify as characteristic of Victorian women, she longs to fly away, 'but as I happen to be a woman instead of a bird, as I have ties at home . . . and as, moreover, I have no wings like a dove to fly away . . . why I must stay at home'. (L 8). Her second publication was a contribution to *Howitt's Visits to Remarkable Places* (1839), and she never lost the urge 'to be off'. Later she did manage increasingly to escape from 'dear old dull ugly smoky grim grey Manchester' (L 384). There were family holidays at Silverdale, Lancashire, and in the Lake District, and in the last ten years of her life she travelled all over Europe, writing travelogue journalism, with one or more daughters, though never her husband, who took his holidays alone. It is at first merely amusing to read her explanation of how he needs ' "entire freedom from responsibility" ' which he could not have if he had the charge of any of us, and of our luggage' (L 490), knowing that she had conveyed herself, daughters, servants and *impedimenta* round Europe for years with perfect competence. But since William can hardly have been ignorant of his wife's abilities, this bit of disingenuousness (on both their parts) suggests the difficulty of overcoming, as a pair, in public, problems which they could cope with as individuals. The trouble with travelling *en famille* was not that Mrs Gaskell couldn't cope but that, with Mr Gaskell present, she wouldn't be allowed to.

Quite contradictory views have been taken of their marriage. A.W. Ward sees it as 'one of unbroken happiness . . . she was able to identify her interests completely with those of her husband' (K I: xxi); Aina Rubenius sees William as a definite constraint on his wife's career. The truth seems to be that they led fairly separate lives, conforming to the pattern described by Carroll Smith-Rosenberg (1975: 9). William was not crudely authoritarian, and Elizabeth described herself on one occasion as 'coward enough to wish that we were back in the darkness where obedience was the only seen duty of women' (L 69). Personally, he was an engaging man, with a 'bright and cheerful mind' (quoted in Gérin 1976: 265; L 489); he was a good teacher and much relied on in the community. His life was as busy as hers, and despite sympathetic views on most subjects, it is clear, from Letter 570 for instance, that they did not impinge on one another much in daily life. Although this left her with freedom of scope, however, it also deprived her of William's day-to-day support. Letter 16 (1841) reveals his almost pathological avoidance of anxiety about his children's health; he 'won't allow me ever to talk to him about anxieties, while it would be SUCH A RELIEF often'. His unavailability creates in her not only present stress but also fears for the future. Knowing 'that dear William feeling most kindly towards his children, is yet most reserved in *expressions* of either affection or sympathy', and convinced that her daughter needs 'the sunshine of love & tenderness' to prevent her from becoming 'sullen & deceitful', Elizabeth begs William's sister, Anne, to shed some womanly warmth on their children in the event of her death. The painful isolation expressed in this letter was undoubtedly a personal source for Elizabeth Gaskell's insistent efforts to promote, through her writing, the closer involvement of men with the care of their children.

Financially, they were never affluent, though Elizabeth's earnings enabled her to travel and eventually to buy the Hampshire house where she died. William's name is invoked in all the early financial transactions – as Gérin points out, a married woman could not have a bank account in her own name (Gérin 1976: 261) – but later she must have overcome this difficulty and in 1865 bought and furnished the Hampshire house without her husband knowing.

Elizabeth Gaskell's attitude to 'women's role' can be seen clearly in her treatment of her four daughters, born between 1834 and 1846 (her only son, Willie, died in 1845 at a year old). From 1835 to 1838 she kept a diary recording the progress of her eldest daughter, Marianne, which contrasts sharply with the more normal Victorian dogma of 'spare the rod and spoil the child'. She watched and noted Marianne's peculiarities of temperament and need, and rather than punishing bad behaviour, tried to remove its cause – such as hunger or fatigue (*MD*: 14). Her aim is to produce rationality, not obedience. Hence she never promises anything which can't be fulfilled, producing 'a pretty good idea of giving up a present pleasure to secure a future one, feeling sure that the promise will be performed' (p. 26). At 4 years old, Marianne is left to make small moral judgements for herself (38), and later the letters show how all the daughters were expected to make reliable judgements in their dealings with other people. Augustus Hare noted Elizabeth Gaskell's 'extreme courtesy and deference to her own daughters' (1896, quoted in Selig 1977: 111), while Charlotte Brontë, with her experience as a

governess, was astonished at their spontaneous kind-
ness (*LCB*: 457–8). Noddings notes that creative children
often have parents who show 'respect for the child and
confidence in his ability to do what was appropriate'
(Noddings 1984: 73).

As a general rule, Gaskell avoided judging for others: 'I
strive more and more against deciding whether any
other person is doing right or wrong' (*L* 424). This
principle links her backwards with Mary Wollstonecroft
– 'definite rules can never apply to indefinite circumstances' (*The Wrongs of Woman* [1798] 1976: 198) – and
forwards to Noddings, who advocates an ethic which
'does not attempt to reduce the need for human
judgement with a series of "Thou shalts" and "Thou shalt
nots"' (Noddings 1984: 25). The need for clear judgement led her to take her daughters' intellectual opinions
seriously, and she warns Marianne against careless
partisanship in politics: 'That is one reason why so many
people dislike that women should meddle with politics
. . . that women are apt to take up a thing without being
even able to state their reasons clearly' (*L* 93). She
specifies a stiff course of reading in political economy
before Marianne shall 'again give a decided opinion on a
subject on which you can at present know nothing'.

On the other hand, the letters reveal what Carroll
Smith-Rosenberg calls 'an intimate mother–daughter
relationship' based on 'an apprenticeship system' in
which mothers 'carefully trained daughters in the arts of
housewifery and motherhood' (Smith-Rosenberg 1975:
16). All the Gaskell daughters were expected to
understand the work of the household (*L* 16a) and to
take charge on occasion. None was educated with a
specific career in mind, though Elizabeth supported
Meta when (in 1854) she wanted to be a nurse (*L* 217).
On the other hand, there was no hint of the marriage

market; Meta was supported when she broke her engagement, and Marianne when she was engaged against the wishes of her fiancé's parents. In Letter 453 Elizabeth Gaskell affirms that, apart from the wish for children, 'an unmarried life may be to the full as happy' as a married one.

She never openly speaks of sexuality and desire; even now, a married woman will be more inhibited in this by her knowledge that such pronouncements will be linked to the one man she may wish to protect or placate. For Elizabeth Gaskell, this reticence was reinforced not only by Victorian ideology but by also by the conscious conviction, which she shared with Mary Wollstonecraft, that sexual attraction is too unpredictable, evanescent and uncontrollable to form more than an incidental part of a rational life. We can only speculate about the information and attitudes she shared with her daughters in private, but the letters dealing with Meta's broken engagement suggest an anxious female solidarity (it was her fiancé's sisters who revealed to Meta their brother's faults) behind a determined public silence. If the ultimate cause of the breach had some sexual component, as seems likely, it is ironic that Elizabeth Gaskell identifies as the immediate cause his failure to explain a falsehood (L 421a). The articulation of sexuality is the one issue which, in Elizabeth Gaskell's writing, strains the Unitarian ethic of truth-telling beyond its ideological limits. Even in *Wives and Daughters* she fails to confront the paradox behind the question whether 'wise parents ever directly speak of what . . . cannot be put into word's (R: 43).

Two of her daughters married; Meta and Julia lived together after their mother's death and were much respected for their active philanthropy. Their mother was intensely concerned that they should give one another sisterly support (*L* 330) and also that they should have dignity and security as single women. She drove herself to finish *Wives and Daughters* to raise money for the Alton house, which was planned not just as a retirement home for her husband (Wright 1965: 207) but as a refuge for her unmarried daughters (*L* 439a, 583).

As a woman, Elizabeth Gaskell was not an obvious innovator, but her life shows how, in favourable circumstances, the doctrine of 'separate spheres' did allow 'a specifically female world' to develop (Smith-Rosenberg 1975: 9), which offered scope for energetic self-determination and female bonding. Her education of her daughters was remarkable for its time in that she allowed their natures to develop rather than imposing patterns on them. Her life, like her work, shows her urgent wish that men and women should both combine rational responsibility with loving care.

2 The Writer

So far I have dealt with Elizabeth Gaskell as a 'relative creature', defined by her status as daughter, wife and mother, and I have tried to stress the enriching rather than the cramping aspects of these roles. But there is no avoiding the serious tension faced by a Victorian woman who tried to be more than a relative creature. Even so domestic a decision as choosing a house prompted Elizabeth Gaskell to realise that she had 'a great number of ' "Mes" ':

One of my mes is, I do believe, a true Christian – (only people call her socialist and communist), another of my mes is a wife and mother. . . . Then again I've another self with a full taste for beauty and convenience. . . . How am I to reconcile all these warring members? I try to drown myself (my *first* self,) by saying it's Wm who is to decide . . . only that does not quite do'. (*L* 69 [1850])

Earlier in the same year she wrote a long letter to Tottie Fox trying to sort out her opposing roles; she would then have had four children aged 4 to 13; *Mary Barton* and some short stories were written and *Cranford* was in progress:

> One thing is pretty clear, *Women*, must give up living an artist's life, if home duties are to be paramount. It is different with men, whose home duties are so small a part of their life. However . . . assuredly a blending of the two is desirable. (Home duties and the development of the Individual I mean), . . . but the difficulty is where and when to make one set of duties subserve and give place to the other. I have no doubt that the cultivation of each tends to keep the other in a healthy state, – my grammar is all at sixes and sevens I have no doubt but never mind if you can pick out my meaning. (*L 68*)

The next day she tries to make the necessary distinction. Self-development is 'unholy' if it is only selfish, but if we can 'find out what we are sent into the world to do, and define it and make it clear to ourselves, (that's *the* hard part)', then it becomes a duty to 'forget ourselves in our work' (*L* 68). Carol Gilligan (1977) sees this emphasis on duty, and difficulty in legitimising self-fulfilment, as peculiar to women's moral reasoning. In interviews with modern American women she identifies three stages of women's consciousness, from the self-centredness of youth through the self-sacrifice of conventional woman-hood to a state in which 'obligation extends to include the self as well as others' and 'the disparity between selfishness and responsibility is reconciled' (Gilligan 1977: 506).

Elizabeth Gaskell, theoretically embracing this third stage, is vividly aware of its practical difficulties. In *The Life of Charlotte Brontë* she notes how the publication of *Jane Eyre* split Charlotte Brontë's existence 'into two parallel currents – her life as Currer Bell, the author; her life as Charlotte Brontë, the woman'. The 'separate duties' were

> not impossible, but difficult to be reconciled. When a man becomes an author . . . another merchant or lawyer, or doctor, steps into his vacant place, and probably does as well as he. But no other can take up the quiet, regular duties of the daughter, the wife, or the mother . . . a woman's principal work in life is hardly left to her own choice; nor can she drop the domestic charges devolving on her . . . for the exercise of the most splendid talents that were ever bestowed. And yet she must not shrink from the extra responsibility implied by the very fact of her possessing such talents (*LCB:* 334)

Letter 515, a long letter to a would-be woman writer burdened with small children, is often quoted to 'prove' that Elizabeth Gaskell approved of the separation of literary and domestic activities (e.g. Gérin 1976: 54; Stone 1980: 141). She advises the woman that she will write better when she is 40 and the children grown up. Chapple notes the apparent disingenuousness of this advice – 'she must have been writing *Mary Barton* when Julia was a baby' (Chapple 1980: 125) – but the letter as a whole is clearly pragmatic in intention; the woman is so poor that she has not the resources to 'blend' roles, and Elizabeth Gaskell very practically addresses herself to remedying what is 'in [her] own power' – 'I hope . . . you soap & soak your dirty clothes well for some hours before beginning to wash. . . . Did you ever try a tea-cup full of *hop-tea* . . . a very simple tonic'. Above all, 'have you no sister or relation . . . no older friend?' In this context the advice about deferring authorship is not ideological prescription but a recognition that even without writing, this woman is 'overwhelmed with all [she has] to do'.

Elizabeth Gaskell herself was more successful at blending the two selves; she can use her education to make a joke out of domestic frustration when she says, 'the little ones come down upon us like the Goths on Rome' (*L* 68), and on the other hand nursery stories provide material to make serious points in her novels about the infantilisation of Victorian girls (see below, Chs. 9 and 10). Activities like reading and playing charades with the girls kept academic knowledge in contact with daily life. While William kept his study like a citadel, Elizabeth chose to write in the dining-room, with doors in all directions keeping her in touch with the flow of activity in the house. Adrienne Rich points out that 'if, in trying to join the common world of men, . . . we split ourselves off from the common life of women . . . we lose touch with our real powers and with the essential condition for all fully realised work: community' (Rich 1980: 207).

In the process of writing itself, Elizabeth Gaskell dislikes masculine abstraction and emphasises concrete particularities. She urges male correspondents to give 'little details which it is "beneath the dignity of man" to put on paper' (*L* 409). To W.J. Fox she appeals for details of his daughter's wedding: 'Who – What, Where, Wherefore, Why – oh! do be a woman, and give me all possible details' (*L* 419). The urgency is not trivial; details are necessary to make narrative interesting (*L* 240), to understand large questions (*L* 384) and to make proper

moral judgements (*L* 424; cf. Noddings 1984: 36). Sara
Ruddick argues that 'this intense, pure, disinterested,
gratuitous, generous attention' to detail is a habit of mind
developed by mothers' necessary attention to their
children (Ruddick 1980: 358). Rooted in love, 'attention'
is nevertheless 'an *intellectual* capacity' producing a mode
of thought different from the abstractions of science
based on repeatable experiments for the purpose of
controlling nature (p. 353). 'Maternal thinking', which
expects change and has nurturance rather than control
as its object, is peculiarly appropriate to studying 'the
changing natures of all peoples and communities' (p.
353) and, 'transformed by feminist consciousness' (p.
356), provides a basis for political action (p. 361).

This ideal receptivity to the detail of daily life needs,
however, a superhuman resilience. In the letter to Tottie
Fox (*L* 68), Elizabeth Gaskell complains of not being able
to think or write clearly, and this is a constant refrain: 'I
must write helter-skelter' (*L* 2); 'I must write . . .
whatever comes into my head (*L* 9); 'I have been so
completely in a "whirl" these two days that I feel as
though I could hardly arrange my thoughts' (quoted in
Chapple 1980: 18). As her writing career progresses,
these laments become heartfelt: 'I . . . was writing away
vigorously at Ruth when the Wedgewoods, Etc. came:
and I was sorry, *very* sorry to give it up my heart being so
full of it, in a way which I can't bring back. That's *that*
(. . .)' (*L* 137). At work on *The Life of Charlotte Brontë*, she has
'the sick wearied feeling of being over-worked; she
would like to write long letters 'only what *can* I do?
The interruptions of home life are never ending; & I
want to read & with the girls' (*L* 308; see also *L* 476a).
Dickens, who published many of her stories, was
puzzled by her 'inability to work steadily at her task'
(Grubb 1943: 97), but the reason is clear. To Charles

Eliot Norton she replies, 'if I had a library like yours, all undisturbed for hours, how I would write! . . . But you see everybody comes to me perpetually' (L 384). In the last year of her life ill-health and financial pressure produce a rare grumble: 'I *must* save all my health and strength for writing . . . I *am* so badly behindhand in Wives & Daughters . . . I am so sorry to think of your fatigue yesterday love. But . . . you are doing nothing you know while I am writing hard at my book' (L 575a); 'another letter-article for Pall Mall Gaz. *by return* of post – simply impossible – but has to be written *today, before* we go to James Reiss's, 1/2 p 3 – Oh dear! I *am* nearly killed' (L 582). The full text of these letters reveals the degree of strain involved in 'blending' her 'selves'. The wonder is, not that she dropped dead from heart failure, but that *Wives and Daughters* was written at all.

As well as practical difficulties, there were the more subtle strains of social disapproval. Sandford describes the common idea of the woman writer: 'The female pedant appears in a disordered dress, and with inky fingers; and fancies that the further she is removed from feminine grace, the nearer she approaches to manly vigour' (Sandford 1831: 22). Geraldine Jewsbury reports that people 'are beginning to be mildly pained for Mr "Mary Barton". And one lady said to me . . . "I don't think authoresses ought ever to marry", and then proceeded to eulogise Mr Gaskell' (Chapple 1980: 43). Elaine Showalter comments:

> Feminine novelists responded to these innuendos of inferiority . . . not by protest but by vigorous demonstration of their domestic felicity. They worked hard to present their writing as an extension of their feminine role . . . it was essential that the writing be carried out in the home, and that it be only one among the numerous and interruptible household tasks of the true woman. (Showalter 1977: 85)

Showalter argues, moreover, that 'because they were so susceptible to the self-doubt engendered by the ideal, most Victorian women writers also conspicuously repudiated the feminist movement' (Gornick and Moran 1971: 461). The passionate support which Elizabeth Gaskell felt for fellow-women went towards proving their impugned femininity. She wrote *The Life of Charlotte Brontë* to 'make the world... honour the woman as much as they have admired the writer' (*L* 241). She emphasises Charlotte Brontë's domestic trials – Branwell deranged, father autocratic, sisters fragile – in order to emphasise her strength in domestic situations (*LCB*: 305) and to excuse what was called 'coarseness' in her writing. Attacking the anonymous *Quarterly* reviewer, Elizabeth Gaskell uses a rhetorical style which betrays her extreme sensitivity to the charge:

> Has he striven through long weeping years to find excuses for the lapse of an only brother . . . compelled into . . . familiarity with the vices that his soul abhors? . . . If through all these dark waters the scornful reviewer have passed clear . . . still, even then let him pray with the Publican rather than judge with the Pharisee. (*LCB*: 360)

This sensitivity led Elizabeth Gaskell to stress every evidence to the contrary; she is delighted with one of Charlotte Brontë's letters which 'showed a nice feminine sense of confidence & pleasure in protection – chaperonage – whatever you like to call it; which is a piece of womanliness (as opposed to the common ideas of her being a "strong-minded emancipated" woman) which I should like to bring out' (*L* 326). She omits any reference to Charlotte Brontë's passionate love for M. Heger, and, reporting her refusal of Mr Nicholls's proposal, she comments, 'Thus quietly and modestly did she, on whom such hard judgements had been passed by ignorant reviewers, receive this vehement, passionate declaration of love, – thus thoughtfully for her father, and unselfishly for herself, put aside all consideration of how she should reply, excepting as he wished' (*LCB*: 491; see also *L* 314, 328).

In general, the more consciously Elizabeth Gaskell wished to vindicate another woman, the more she stressed that woman's orthodox 'womanliness'. Thus *Ruth*, which has a clearly contentious subject, struck even some contemporary readers as cautious and conservative, while *Wives and Daughters*, in which she was 'off guard' as to the 'woman question', makes a thorough critique of female socialisation.

The threat of censure affected her writing in minute ways. Her letters are normally an uninhibited torrent of detail, wry humour and disconcerting juxtaposition, suggesting a strong, independent personality; but even here she is made to feel self-conscious; 'When I had finished my last letter Willm looked at it, and said it was *"slip-shod"* – and seemed to wish me not to send it . . . the sort of consciousness that Wm may any time and does generally see my letters makes me not write so naturally & heartily as I think I should do' (*L* 13 [1838]). As late as 1857 she is reluctant to write to a stranger: 'it is so hard to me to write a proper letter; with Dear Sir in the right place, & verbs agreeing with their nominatives, & {agreeing with [*cancelled*]} governing – their accusatives; and it is letters of that kind I dread receiving, because of the knowledge of grammar, & good pens required to answer them' (*L* 384). Her published writing brought outward respect but, she suspects, hasn't changed real opinions: 'Dr Holland once called a letter of mine "a heterogeneous mass of nonsense". But that was before I wrote Mary B – he would not *say* so now' (*L* 195). In such an exuberant and capable writer these signs of insecurity are poignant, but evidently real. The mere prospect of speaking in public reduces her to incoherence: 'I could not – physically *could* not, I believe, speak out more than a blurting sentence of abuse, tantamount to a box on the ear, – a "That's a downright falsehood", I might say, – or even *worse*, not *more*. – It is different when speaking as the character in a {s} story – or even as the author of a book' (*L* 171). Evidently, fictional impersonation freed her from some sense of oppression entailed in using the language of formal public discourse. When the Brontës attempted this sort of masculine colour, she said it made their novels '"technically false", even "[made] their writing squint"' (quoted in Gilbert and Gubar 1979: 70–1). Elizabeth Gaskell avoided this 'male mimicry' as far as possible, refusing, for instance, the language of political economy in *Mary Barton* (*MB*: 38). But she could not avoid all dealings with the public world, and it is characteristic that she should use her experience of book-publishing, for example, to help other women: 'I would be so glad to help them. . . . I never had anyone to help me, & found [things] all out by accident . . . & I think other women may be like me' (*L* 328). In *The Life of Charlotte Brontë* she notices Charlotte's 'inexperience in the ways of the world', which led to her not receiving a reply from a publisher because she had not enclosed a postage-stamp (*LCB*: 316–7).

The need for mutual female support may explain her fascination with the French *salon* tradition described in *French Life* and *Company Manners*. She planned a biography of Mme de Sévigné and writes enthusiastically about Mme Mohl's modern *salons* (*K* I: xxxvii). Marks and de Courtivron note that only in France 'have groups of women come together with the express purpose of criticising and reshaping the official male language and, through it, male manners and male power' (Marks and de Courtivron 1982: 6). In particular Elizabeth Gaskell admired the story-telling tradition of Mme de Sablé's circle (*K3*: 508), and in *Round the Sofa*, a story-cycle with linking commentary, she demonstrates an oral tradition stretching back from the young narrative persona through two intermediaries to Fanny Burney. The women 'round the sofa' encourage one another in literary ventures and even, under the guise of story-telling, pass comment on social and political issues. Many of Elizabeth Gaskell's stories, like *Sylvia's Lovers*, are framed to emphasise the way in which experience is handed on and affects later generations. *The Grey Woman*, like Wollstonecraft's *The Wrongs of Woman*, is a mother's autobiographical letter warning her daughter of the dangers of marriage.

Elizabeth Gaskell's insecurity in handling the language of 'high culture' led her to project a falsely unintellectual image of herself which has been accepted by critics of all kinds. Yet she is likely to have read her father's articles and other works on political economy (Stevenson 1824–5; *L*93; Hopkins 1931:60); the footnotes to modern editions of her work show an impressive range of references to classical and modern literature; and in *The Life of Charlotte Brontë* she puts as much emphasis on Charlotte's intellectual capacity as on her domestic docility (*LCB*: 139, 152), giving a lengthy analysis of Charlotte's studies in Brussels (pp. 225–39) and noting the books and literary questions discussed in her letters (pp. 338, 428, 507, 512).

Elizabeth Gaskell herself had a fairly good education for a girl of her time (see Gérin 1976: 23–32) and early in her marriage embarked on literary collaboration with her husband. Together they wrote lectures on the English poets for working men (*L* 4) (which William, of course, delivered) and planned 'Sketches Among the

Poor' in the style of Crabbe (L 12). Letter 9 contains a parody of a Johnsonian sentence, suggesting a mind moving relatively at ease in the literary heritage. Yet her culturally induced diffidence has combined with the 'double critical standard' to ensure that the intertextuality of Elizabeth Gaskell's works has been ignored. Critics seldom comment on her allusions, and yet they are often a vital clue in aligning or dissociating the text from culturally transmitted ideologies. The hero of *The Doom of the Griffiths*, caught up in an Oedipal drama at home, reads *Oedipus Tyrannus* on a Welsh hillside (*K5:* 249), and in *Lizzie Leigh* the mother's submission to her husband is explained by Milton's 'He for God only, she for God in him' (*K2:* 206).

The Bible is a major source of Elizabeth Gaskell's allusion, which has been assumed to signal 'a simple undenominational piety' (Cecil 1934: 198). Here, however, are striking examples of Showalter's 'double-voiced discourse', embodying both muted and dominant. In *Lizzie Leigh*, for instance, often read as a saccharine tale (e.g. Fryckstedt 1982: 192–3), Elizabeth Gaskell uses not the Magdalen but the Progidal Son as her analogy for the fallen woman, drawing attention to the then normal differential of blame for male and female sinners; the prodigal eats the fatted calf while the magdalen washes Christ's feet with her tears.

Behind many of Elizabeth Gaskell's ideas on the education and social role of women lies the tradition of rational feminism as expressed by Mary Wollstonecraft. In spite of the incongruity between Wollstonecraft's Jacobinical, free-love image and Mrs Gaskell's demure matronliness, there is considerable congruity of ideas. Both believe that women must be treated as rational and responsible because subordination is contrary to Christianity and because only rational beings can be capable mothers. Both deplore the education of girls only to be pleasing to men, and attack the same conduct-book writers – Dr Gregory and Lord Chesterfield in particular. Both believe that working women are often more 'rational beings' than 'fine ladies'; both believe that sexual love causes more mischief than fulfilment and that friendship is a more rational basis for relationships of all kinds (Tomalin 1974: 106). Both believe that while women must be seen as citizens, their 'peculiar duties' lie in the family (W: 70). And, as I shall argue in the next chapter, both make the same distinctions between justice and the law. We know that Elizabeth Gaskell knew Wollstonecraft's writing (L 25a); Wollstonecraft also moved in Unitarian circles (Holt 1938: 110, 147) at a time when Elizabeth Gaskell's father was himself a Unitarian minister (Gérin 1976: 3). Elizabeth Gaskell possibly avoids public reference to Wollstonecraft to avoid appearing a 'strong-minded woman' or being associated with sexual freedom. Even feminists 'abandoned Wollstonecraft so as not to bring down upon their own heads the opprobrium of being thought sexually wanton' (Brody, in Spender 1983: 41).

Because ideological pressure makes Elizabeth Gaskell uneasy both in her use of 'masculine', 'public' language and in aligning herself with 'strong-minded' women, we can expect that she will be least authentic when she feels herself most exposed. A superficial reading of her controversial novels tends to foreground her orthodoxy; here we must use the perspectives discussed in Chapter 1 (2 iv–v) to reveal her 'double-voiced discourse'. Her less notorious stories and essays, however, offer access to her opinions that is often simple and direct, and sometimes strikingly symbolic.

Chapter Three

Two Nations and Separate Spheres: Class and Gender in Elizabeth Gaskell's Work

The society in which Elizabeth Gaskell lived and wrote was intersected horizontally by class and vertically by gender divisions. Critics have created a divided image of her work by focusing on one or other of these axes – 'industrial' or 'domestic' – and we can simply, but radically, revise this view by considering their inter-action. I want to begin by drawing examples from Elizabeth Gaskell's lesser-known fiction, in which the issues are often very clear, but which critics have less completely labelled and categorised; this discussion will then serve as a context for a rereading of the familiar works in subsequent chapters.

What emerges from her work as a whole is that, at subsistence level, gender divisions are blurred: women exercise responsibility; men give basic nurturance. In the middle class, ideology heightens differentiation, producing infantilised women and authoritarian men.

1 *Working Women*

Because Elizabeth Gaskell's studies of working-class life are read as 'industrial' novels, criticism has focused on factory-workers like John Barton and Nicholas Higgins. Her work as a whole, however, highlights working women – not just factory workers like Bessy Higgins but seamstresses, milliners, washerwomen, 'chars', a tailor, beekeepers, farmers, housewives and domestic servants. Her very first publication is a verse portrait of an old working woman ('Sketches Among the Poor', K1: xxii–xxv). Her first published story, *Libbie Marsh's Three Eras* (1847), is about the friendship of an unmarried seamstress and a widowed washerwoman. These stories are remarkable for their focus on the physical detail of working-class life. Her Sunday-school stories, *Hand and Heart* (1849) and *Bessy's Troubles at Home* (1852), bring home the sheer effort required to produce the simplest results – a cup of tea, for instance – in the working-class homes of the 1840s (K3: 548–9, 534).

Yet work is not seen primarily as a hardship in these stories but as a means to self-sufficiency and mutual support. In *The Well of Pen-Morfa* (1850) an unmarried mother supports herself by beekeeping; in *The Manchester Marriage* (1858) a widow, her mother-in-law and their servant keep themselves by running a boarding-house; in *The Grey Woman* (1861) a servant supports her former mistress by working as a tailor. As Anna Walters says in her splendid introduction to the Pandora *Four Short Stories* 'we are left as so often in Gaskell's writing with the impression of what women *can* do rather than the reverse' (P: 14).

Perhaps the most impressive example of self-sufficiency is that of Susan Dixon, the Cumbrian 'stateswoman' in *Half A Lifetime Ago* (1855). As manager and later owner of the farm where she works alongside the labourers, she seems to epitomise Mary Wollstonecraft's ideal: 'how many women . . . waste life away the prey of discontent, who might have practised as physicians, regulated a farm, managed a shop, and stood erect, supported by their own industry' (W: 163). Susan's life, however, is grim and lonely until she takes to live with her the widow and orphans of her former lover; 'and so it fell out', the story succinctly ends, 'that the latter days of Susan Dixon's life were better than the former' (CP: 102).

Although three of Elizabeth Gaskell's best-known novels (*Mary Barton*, *North and South* and *Wives and Daughters*) end with a love-match, most of the short stories, together with *Cranford*, *Ruth*, *Sylvia's Lovers* and *Cousin Phillis*, stress the unreliability of sexual love and the durability of female friendships. Libbie Marsh and Margaret Hall agree to live together; Mrs Leigh sets up house with her 'fallen' daughter Lizzie; Nest Gwynne in *The Well of Pen-Morfa*, betrayed by her lover, takes in an idiot woman 'on the parish'; in *My Lady Ludlow* (1858) an aristocratic lady 'adopts' half-a-dozen needy young gentlewomen; in *A Dark Night's Work* (1863) Ellinor sets up house with her former governess; in *The Grey Woman* (1861) a servant disguises herself as a man and lives with her former mistress as her husband.

Female alliances occur naturally in the working-class, where needs are urgent and neighbours close by, but for Elizabeth Gaskell's middle-class women, help comes less from friends than from servants. Like Mary Wollstonecraft, she believed that good sense and heroism were more likely where people were forced to confront real crises. 'With respect to virtue', says Wollstonecraft, 'I have seen most in low life . . . gentle-women are too indolent to be actively virtuous' (W: 84).

The revolutionary function of domestic servants in Elizabeth Gaskell's work has been largely over-looked; critics seem blinkered by the stage convention that servants are comic, colourful 'characters'. Yet they provide practical, moral and psychological decision in situations which are sometimes deadly serious. Adrienne Rich argues that 'because the conditions of life for many poor women demand a fighting spirit for sheer physical survival, such mothers have sometimes been able to give their daughters something to be valued far more highly than full-time mothering' (Rich 1977: 247). Elizabeth Gaskell's middle-aged servants are generally childless, but they function as 'fighting mothers' for the middle-class woman in their care. It is Peggy who sustains Susan Dixon, and Betty Cousin Phillis, after the defection of lovers; it is Sally who teaches Ruth to survive by putting effort into proximate tasks; Miss Monro, the governess in *A Dark Night's Work*, not only works for Ellinor but stops her going mad; Norah, in *The Manchester Marriage*, takes on the moral dilemma about disclosing a family secret; in *Cranford*, Martha becomes her former mistress's landlady to save her from penury; and Nancy is the moral backbone of the Brown family in *The Moorland Cottage* (1862). When Mrs Buxton in that tale tells stories of saints and heroines to the little girls, she includes servants (K2: 296).

All these situations blur class boundaries, and although Elizabeth Gaskell herself had a number of servants, her behaviour throughout her life defines their relationship as one of function rather than immutable class distinction. When Marianne was a baby, she wrote, 'we have lost our servant Betsy. . . . But we still keep her as a friend, and she has been to stay with us several weeks this autumn' (MD: 28). After all the girls were grown up their governess, Hearn, stayed on as 'a dear good valuable *friend'* (*L* 570). In *French Life* Elizabeth Gaskell praises the French habit of living in flats because 'there is the moral advantage of uniting mistresses and maids in a more complete family bond.... [a] pleasant kind of familiarity ... which does not breed contempt, in spite of proverbs' (*K7*: 609). A contemporary conduct-book, declaring it 'highly improper for young people to associate with their servants' (*NFI*: 367), emphasises her unconventionality.

In *The Old Nurse's Story* (1852) this theme is given a 'gothic' treatment. A 5-year-old girl, the youngest of a decayed aristocratic family, is poised between the drawing-room, occupied by a silent great-aunt, and the warm life of the kitchen. Tempted to her death by a phantom child, she is rescued by her nurse. Under the supernatural surface we can read the author's resistance to aristocratic values – patrilineal pride of possession, sexual rivalry and the ethic of revenge. Hester the nurse and the other working people provide an alternative pattern for personal relationships, unstructured by kinship but united by common nurturance and co-operation.

The care of children is Elizabeth Gaskell's crucial test of moral values; seen as a communal duty (though undertaken by individuals), it takes precedence over all other responsibilities and is never restricted to biological mothers or conventional households. Servants act as 'fighting mothers' to their charges; widows and un-married mothers cope alone; Libbie Marsh devotes herself to a neighbour's child; Susan Palmer, in *Lizzie Leigh* (1850), brings up a baby thrust at her in the street; Bessy looks after her brothers and sisters; Miss Galindo, in *My Lady Ludlow*, adopts her dead lover's child; Lady Ludlow adopts a houseful of girls; in *Mary Barton*, Alice Wilson brings up her brother's son. Everywhere in

Elizabeth Gaskell's work the maternal instinct flourishes, inside and outside marriage, with and without biological ties.

2   Nurturing Men

By stressing woman's common need for economic self-sufficiency, supportive friendships and maternal roles, Elizabeth Gaskell's stories blur distinctions between classes and between married and unmarried women. Even more unexpected is that her close acquaintance with working-class life leads her to represent gender divisions as indistinct. Early in her marriage she writes to Mary Howitt:

> As for the Poetry of Humble Life, that, even in a town, is met with on every hand . . . we constantly meet with examples of the beautiful truth in that passage of 'The Cumberland Beggar':
>
> > 'Man is dear to man; the poorest poor
> > Long for some moments in a weary life
> > When they can know and feel that they have been,
> > Themselves, the fathers and the dealers out
> > Of some small blessings; have been kind to such
> > As needed kindness, for this simple cause,
> > That we have all of us a human heart' [sic]
> >
> > (L 12)

In the crowded necessities of 'the poorest poor', acts of kindess were performed by whoever was nearest, and every home was 'an essential mutual-aid society' (Weeks 1981: 68). In *Mary Barton* two men visit a family where the husband is delirious and the wife and children starving:

rough, tender nurses as they were, [they] lighted the fire.
.... [Barton] began, with the useful skill of a working-man,
to make some gruel; and . . . forced one or two drops
between her clenched teeth.... Wilson... had soothed, and
covered the man many a time; he had fed and hushed the
little child, and spoken tenderly to the woman (*MB*: 99–100,
102)

Wilson's first appearance is 'tenderly carrying a baby in
arms', and almost the first words Barton speaks are,
'"now, Mrs Wilson, give me the baby"' (*MB*: 42). Similarly, Job Legh's account of two elderly men bringing a
baby from London to Manchester, though comic, is full
of tenderness (*MB*: 147–153).

Elizabeth Gaskell's Sunday-school stories are where
we would expect to find most explicit didacticism about
social role-playing, and each of them stresses gender-
role reversal. Bessy learns 'the difficult arts of family life'
from an older brother, and in *Hand and Heart*, the
'ministering angel' is a little boy. Tom Fletcher creates
the sort of domestic peace we associate with Dickens's
child-heroines; when orphaned he derives comfort from
nursing his aunt's baby (*K3*: 554), and eventually he
reforms the whole rowdy, quarrelsome household:

His uncle sometimes said he was more like a girl than a boy
. . . but . . . he really respected him for the very qualities
which are most truly 'manly'; for the courage with which he
dared to do what was right, and the quiet firmness with
which he bore many kinds of pain. (*K3*: 555)

In *The Half-Brothers* the slow-witted Godfrey gives his life
to save the brother entrusted to him by their dying
mother, protecting him from freezing with the warmth
of his own body; like Tom Fletcher's, his action is both
'manly' and physically succouring. Elizabeth Gaskell's

middle-class heroes are often doctors, who have professionalised the nurturing role.

Gender roles in these tales are not only blurred in general but shift according to circumstances. When the hero in *Six Weeks at Heppenheim* is nursed by the servant Thekla, her 'support was as firm as a man's could have been' (K7: 367), yet when she is distressed he invites her to ' "tell me all about it, as you would to your mother" ' (p. 374). Later Thekla, though 'strong as a man', is fed like a baby by Herr Muller, while her hands are busy nursing his little boy (p. 402).

The parental imperative is at the basis of Elizabeth Gaskell's unorthodox treatment of gender roles. Parents, whether mothers or fathers, need to be both responsible and caring. In *Mary Barton* and *Sylvia's Lovers* political activism in both men and women rises directly from thwarted parental love. As a political writer, Elizabeth Gaskell has attracted condescending criticism from critics who see 'loving-kindness' as a lame alternative to political action. Yet Eli Zaretsky, in *Capitalism, the Family and Personal Life*, writes:

> Part of our problem in dealing with these questions is that socialists tend to hold conservative and inadequate psychological conceptions, according to which human beings are essentially thought and labour. But the human need to love and be loved is as fundamental as the need to work. We need a more tentative and experimental attitude toward emotional life. (Zaretsky 1976: 142)

Whereas Zaretsky sees personal life as 'one problem among many' (p. 142), materialist feminists see it as fundamental. Dinnerstein, Chodorow and O'Brien, for instance, argue that the inclusion of men in primary child-care would undermine the aggressive masculinity which perpetuates capitalism (Chodorow 1978: 186; see above, Ch. 1 (2vi). Elizabeth Gaskell's enthusiasm for nurturing men bears the same relationship to this developed theory as early Utopian socialism bears to Marxist analysis of class; as Mary O'Brien puts it, 'Utopians were so innocent of the true nature of class struggle that they even called on the ruling class for help in destroying itself' (O'Brien 1981: 22). Elizabeth Gaskell extrapolated, from her observation of men on the edge of subsistence, to a general vision of masculine self-deconstruction which initially included a good deal of wish-fulfilment. The optimistic paternalism of *Mary Barton* gives way to a more guarded attitude to men in *North and South* and a more complete focus on women in *Wives and Daughters*. Despite her uncertainty about the means, however, Elizabeth Gaskell's vision of the caring father remains a valid and vital goal, which modern feminists with sharper analytic tools are just beginning to recognise.

3 The Infantilisation of Girls

While necessity eroded gender division, middle-class leisure elaborately reinforced the doctrine of separate spheres. Role-reversal appears ludicrous:

> a husband who should personally direct the proceedings of the housekeeper and the cook, and intrude into the petty arrangements of daily economy, would appear . . . as ridiculous as if he were to assume to himself the habiliments of his wife, or occupy his mornings with her needles and work-bags. (*NFI*, 1824: 69)

The New Female Instructor, or Young Woman's Guide to Domestic Happiness, Being an Epitome of all the Acquirements Necessary to Form the Female Character . . . went through six editions between 1811 and 1836, the period of Elizabeth Gaskell's girlhood. It begins unequivocally with the doctrine that women's role is to please men: 'In their forms lovely, in their manners soft and engaging, they can infuse . . . a thousand nameless sweets into society, which, without them, would be insipid, and barren of sentiment and feeling' (p. 1).

This stereotype contrasts strongly with Elizabeth Gaskell's working heroines; Libbie Marsh is so plain that she is jokingly advised to get a job scaring birds (P: 24); Nest Gwynne is crippled, with eyes 'sunk deep down in their hollow, cavernous sockets' (P: 87); Susan Dixon's 'skin was weather-beaten, furrowed, brown, . . . her teeth were gone, and her hair grey and ragged' (CP: 99); Thelka's complexion is 'bronzed and reddened by weather (K7: 364). Even for middle-class women, Elizabeth Gaskell does not see beauty as as asset; she describes Effie Ruskin as 'very close to a charming character; if she had had the small pox she would have been so' (L 195).

Mary Wollstonecraft saw the tradition of educating girls only to please, as responsible for women's narcissism, deviousness, sensuality and irrationality. The conduct-books 'render women more artificial, weak characters, than they would otherwise have been . . . [they] degrade one-half of the human species, and render women pleasing at the expense of every solid virtue' (W: 26). Similarly, Elizabeth Gaskell shows that this ideology distorts parental feeling, making parents protect girls rather than educate them. Mr Wilkins in *A Dark Night's Work* is a rich and doting father but tells the governess to teach Ellinor '"only what a lady should know"' (K7: 415; see also 430, 501), an attitude repeated by Mr Holman and Mr Gibson (below, Chs. 9 and 10). As Peter Cominos points out, although 'a conscious struggle was waged on behalf of their moral purity by overprotective parents and chaperons', the girls themselves were kept 'innocent' and hence irresponsible (Vicinus 1972: 161). But, as these stories show, daughters cannot be protected from every moral decision. Each heroine acquires the strength and knowledge to cope with adult life, often with the help of servants rather than parents, but at unnecessary emotional cost. Elizabeth Gaskell's own daughter, by contrast, was left at 4 years old 'to judge if such an action be right or not . . . [to] exercise her conscience' (*MD*: 38).

The last part of *Morton Hall* is an attack on conduct-book education; three maiden aunts try out different 'systems' on their niece. The eldest models herself on Lord Chesterfield, whose 'unmanly, immoral system' is, according to Wollstonecraft, second only to Rousseau's in perniciousness: 'instead of preparing young people to encounter the evils of life with dignity, and to acquire wisdom and virtue by the exercise of their own faculties, precepts are heaped upon precepts, and blind obedience required when conviction should be brought home to reason' (*W*: 116-7). Accordingly, Cordelia in *Morton Hall* is subjected to arbitrary rules; she must eat her meals standing, drink cold water before pudding, and never say 'red' or 'stomach-ache' (*K2*: 483). Although Miss Morton poses as a strong-minded woman who despises mere beauty, she is careful that Cordelia preserves her complexion (p. 477). Wollstonecraft points to similar hypocrisy in Dr Gregory's renowned *Legacy to His Daughters*, where daughters are taught that though it is 'indelicate' *obviously* to want to please men, 'it may govern their conduct' (*W*: 36).

Cordelia's second aunt, who educates her 'sensibilities' (*K2*: 478), is subjected to gentle satire which is nevertheless in line with Wollstonecraft's attack on sensibility, which 'naturally relaxes the other powers of the mind, and prevents intellect from attaining that sovereignty which it ought to attain to render a rational creature useful to others' (W: 68).

The third aunt has no system but frightens Cordelia with dogmatic and unpredictable ways. This tale is very light humour, but it shows that Gaskell concurred with the Wollstonecraft thesis that conduct-book education based on obedience or sensibility was debilitating and that the marginalised role of many middle-class women made them into dogmatists, invalids or eccentrics.

4 The Fallibility of Authority

If woman's role was obedience, man's was command. Françoise Basch and Erna Reiss give a staggering account of the legal non-entity of Victorian married women. 'A woman, in law, belonged to the man she married; she was his chattel' (Reiss 1934: 6). In the early part of the period she had no rights over her own body, her children, her earned or inherited income or her place of residence. A husband was even responsible for his wife's debts and crimes. This situation clearly conflicts with Elizabeth Gaskell's Unitarian concept of the rational responsibility of every individual for his or her own conduct.

The facile assumption of much Gaskell criticism has been that she 'looked up to man as her sex's rightful and benevolent master' (Cecil 1934: 198; Duthie 1980: 90). But many of her 'horror' stories depend on the inhuman possibilities of authority. In the early part of *Morton Hall* a sane Royalist lady is consigned to a mad-house by her Puritan husband; in *The Grey Woman* the heroine is married by a well-intentioned father to a man who proves to be a brigand who tortures victims on a heated iron floor; in *French Life* (1864) an aristocratic lady is poisoned, forced from a high window and repeatedly stabbed by her male relatives with the connivance of a priest. In *Lois The Witch* (1859) several hundred people, mostly women, are imprisoned and nineteen executed during the Salem witch hunt with the approval of every authority figure from fathers, guardians and ministers of the Church to judges and politicians. Although Basch claims that 'Mrs Gaskell and the majority of feminist reformers . . . blamed husbands abusing their powers and the law rather than accuse the powers and the law themselves' (Basch 1974: 270), Gaskell returns so often to the abuse of authority that her work as a whole does constitute a challenge to patriarchy itself, which confers on one set of people the right to command, and on another the duty to obey.

There are rather few 'orthodox' families, with father, mother and two or more children, in Elizabeth Gaskell's work, but when they do appear, *paterfamilias* is always a source of oppression and misery. Lizzie Leigh is driven into prostitution when her father disowns her; the Rev. Jenkyns, in *Cranford*, banishes his son Peter for half a lifetime; Mr Bradshaw, in *Ruth*, tyrannises his family. In *The Heart of John Middleton*, the hero begins life as 'Ishmael', the outcast, and only gradually validates his masculine status in the community by proving his ability to earn his living, fight his rivals and support his wife. But whereas as an outcast he had lived in love of his father and fellowship with other poachers, as a church-goer and upholder of the law he lives by the ethic of 'an eye for an eye'.

Bourgeois men in Elizabeth Gaskell's works are not only tyrannical but culpable. Edward in *The Moorland Cottage* and Richard in *Ruth* both exploit positions of trust to embezzle funds; in *The Squire's Story* (1858) the heroine's husband turns out to be a highwayman; Mr Wilkins, a lawyer and the heroine's father in *A Dark Night's Work*, kills his clerk in anger.

Not only individuals, however, but the law itself is fallible. In *The Grey Woman* the heroine escapes her brigand husband but, as an absconding wife, can claim no protection from the law and spends years in flight and disguise. In both *Mary Barton* and *A Dark Night's Work* the courts are ready to execute an innocent man. The whole of *Sylvia's Lovers* is a protracted protest against the legal injustice of the press-gang. Frederick Hale's mutiny against unjust naval officers in *North and South* is surely meant as a redeeming analogy for the workers' riot against the threat of the militia. *An Accursed Race*, dealing with the persecution of the 'Cagots' in France and Spain, shows legalised injustice on the scale of genocide. As Noddings puts it, 'obedience to law is simply not a reliable guide to moral behaviour' (Noddings 1984: 201).

Lady Ludlow exposes the contingent nature of 'the law' when she bursts out ' "Bah! Who makes laws? Such as I, in the House of Lords – such as you, in the House of Commons" ' (*K5*: 38), and repeatedly the stories endorse the distinction between 'justice' and 'the law'. In *The Crooked Branch* (1859) a mother, forced to testify against her son, is seized with a stroke, and her husband tells the court: ' "now yo've truth, and a' th' truth, and I'll leave yo' to th' Judgment o' God for th' way yo've getten at it" ' (*CP*: 238).

The contrast between justice and the law is most developed in *Lois the Witch*, where the authority-structures of a whole nation are complicit in cruel persecution. The story ends with a confession of guilt and fallibility by the judge and jury responsible for the executions. Two other stories also deal with supposed witches: *The Heart of John Middleton* (1850) is set on Pendle Hill, and *The Poor Clare* (1856) in the Trough of Bolland – both districts historically associated with witch hunts – and each concerns an independent old woman whose psychology Elizabeth Gaskell analyses in a realistic way. In *Lois the Witch*, among various psychological determinants of the mass delusion of Salem, she emphasises the gullibility of people who are used to deferring to authority; a powerful preacher like Cotton Mather could influence thousands, and Lois herself begins to wonder whether she is a witch when authoritative voices tell her so. The Unitarian Charles Upham, whose *Lectures on Witchcraft* (1831) were Elizabeth Gaskell's source, attacks 'the leaders of opinion' who constitute 'the law' in its widest sense:

> a physician gave the first impulse to the awful work . . . the judges and officers of the law did what they could to drive on the delusion . . . the clergy were also instrumental in promoting the proceedings. Nay, it must be acknowledged that they took the lead (Upham 1831: 88–9)

Upham concludes that Salem forces everyone to think about 'the cultivation and government of his own moral and intellectual faculties, and . . . the obligations that press on him as a member of society to do what he may to enlighten, rectify and control public sentiment' (p. vi).

The fallibility of 'the law' requires everyone to take moral responsibility for themselves. This position is vehemently endorsed in William Gaskell's sermon 'Unitarian Christians Called to Bear Witness to the Truth' (1862). If we:

> lock up our higher thoughts till infallibility has set its seal upon them . . . priestcraft and intolerance would have

strangled everything like free opinion. . . . The apostle's 'we believe and therefore speak', is applicable to every member of the Church universal who has a mind to think, a heart to feel, and a tongue to utter (W. Gaskell 1862: 5–6)

Emphasis on correctness of creed leads to 'inquisitions, persecutions and miseries without end' (p. 14). The justification for a narrowly defined creed enforced by an authoritarian Church has been the doctrine of original sin, which Gaskell sees as a denial of human reason. Thinking people, told:

> that they sinned in Adam . . . that every new-born infant is responsible for an act committed thousands of years ago . . . feel it no heresy to give this a flat denial. Teach them that it required the blood of his innocent Son to turn aside God's ire and reconcile Him to men, and they say at once then He must be essentially vengeful and unjust. Declare to them that, for the sins of this short life, He consigns myriads of his creatures to everlasting woe, and they call it a mockery to represent this as a Father's mode of dealing with his children. . . . Doctrines like this go right against their natural conscience. Their moral feelings revolt at them (pp. 11–12)

Unitarians believe that every human being has the qualities – reason and love – for self-government and social responsibility. William Gaskell calls for 'a faith which, so far from contradicting, will be in full unison with the best dictates of the heart – which, instead of outraging moral feeling, will "commend itself to every man's conscience . . ."' (p. 19). This doctrine, potentially subversive of the authority not only of the Church but of class and gender, underlies everything Elizabeth Gaskell wrote.

Patriarchal power in Elizabeth Gaskell's tales is shown

as superceding even class power. Although Lucas claim that she presents '"old" families . . . in an exclusively favourable light' (Lucas 1977: 3), and Duthie that she 'honoured . . . the patriarchal pattern' (Duthie 1980: 90), the stories dealing with great houses (*Morton Hall, Crowley Castle, French Life, The Old Nurse's Story*) are a catalogue of torture, madness and lingering death for their women, whose artistocratic status is no defence against masculine power. Theorists like Rousseau argue that the fallibility of male authority only makes a woman's subjection more necessary: 'formed to obey a being so imperfect as man, often full of vices, and always full of faults, she ought to learn betimes even to suffer injustice, and to bear the insults of a husband without complaint' (quoted in *W*: 92). Rousseau is Wollstonecraft's prime target in *A Vindication of the Rights of Woman*, and although by the 1850s Wollstonecraft had fallen into silent neglect, there was still much public debate about women's defenceless position under the law (see Basch 1974: 16–25). Barbara Bodichon and Caroline Norton both wrote books on women and the law in 1854, and Norton, who was quite a close friend of Elizabeth Gaskell (*L*209, 372, 407, 438, 552), was possibly the link between her and Wollstonecraft. Norton's *English Laws for Women in the Nineteenth Century* (1854), largely based on her own sufferings at the hands of her husband, reads like a documentary rerun of Wollstonecraft's novel *Maria, or the Wrongs of Woman* (1798).

When, however, at Bodichon's request, Elizabeth Gaskell signed the 1856 Petition to protect the property of married women, she did so with reservations, saying 'a husband can coax, wheedle, beat or tyrannize his wife out of something and no law whatever will help this that I see' (*L* 276). This statement has been used to suggest that Elizabeth Gaskell was opposed to the 'women's rights' movement (e.g. Thomspon, quoted in Welch 1977: 38; Duthie 1980: 90; Chapple 1980: xiii), but it surely rises from a radical scepticism about the ability of the law to protect women in a society where patriarchal power is entrenched in the most personal relationships. As well as legal enablement, individual women need to strengthen their sense of autonomy, their power to act and speak.

In the writings of Elizabeth Gaskell, as in those of Norton and Wollstonecraft, the actual injuries of women raise less indignation than their induced submission, which makes them less than human, takes responsibility for their fate out of their own hands and denies them the right claimed by William Gaskell for every Christian to 'bear witness to the truth'. For all these writers, public speech is a claim to participate in the symbolic order; obedience is equated with silence. According to Wollstonecraft, 'the being who patiently endures injustice, and silently bears insults, will soon become unjust, or unable to discern right from wrong' (W: 92). To those 'who deem a husband's right so indefeasible, and his title so sacred, that even a wronged wife should keep silence', Caroline Norton replies, 'I resist' (Norton 1854: 2-3).

Similarly, Elizabeth Gaskell's tales often hinge around a change from silent endurance to public speech which changes the status of the speaker from submission to authority. In *Right at Last* (originally called *The Sin of a Father*), a husband endures blackmail rather than suffer the exposure of his father's crime; his wife, finding 'something so weak and poor' in his character, determines 'to rely on herself alone in all cases of emergency' (K7: 290). Maggie, in *The Moorland Cottage*, though brought up to obey her brother, defies him for moral reasons. In *A Dark Night's Work* Ellinor spends years in dread of her father's crime being discovered, believing herself bound to silence by '"filial piety"' (K7: 478); her father tells her to '"stand alone, and bear the sins of thy father"' (p. 510). Eventually, she speaks to protect a friend. 'Bearing witness to the truth', is never, in these tales, a matter of conforming to law, but of judging the circumstances. In *Right at Last* the wife delivers the blackmailer to the law because he tyrannises their lives; in *The Heart of John Middleton* the wife argues against handing over their old enemy as a mere act of vengeance.

Elizabeth Gaskell's tales resoundingly reject Mrs Ellis's maxim that 'a woman's highest duty is so often to suffer and be still (Ellis 1845: 126). In *Lizzie Leigh*, the submissive wife, whose husband 'was truly the interpreter, who stood between God and her' (P: 48) is disillusioned by his rejection of Lizzie, and when their son Will seems about to act likewise, she speaks:

> 'I must speak, and you must listen. I am your mother, and I dare to command you, because I know I am in the right and that God is on my side. . . .' She stood, no longer as the meek, imploring, gentle mother, but firm and dignified, as if the interpreter of God's will. (P: 67).

In *The Well of Pen-Morfa* Nest Gwynne's mother, similarly bold on her daughter's behalf, speaks to her betrayer: '"You *must* tell me." She stood up and spoke in a tone of command' (P: 84). And in *Mary Barton* the outcast prostitute Esther speaks with the authority of experience and the courage of parental concern: '"You must listen to me, Jem Wilson", she said, with almost an accent of command. . . . "You must listen", she said again, authoritatively, "for Mary Barton's sake"' (MB: 208). When Mr Bradshaw in *Ruth* threatens his son with prosecution, his hitherto submissive wife is driven '"to

speak [her] mind, and say to everybody how cruel he is"'
(R: 404), and his daughter defies him to defend her
friend: '"Father! I will speak, I will not keep silence. I will
bear witness to Ruth"' (R: 335).

Religion, in Victorian England, could serve the
ideology of separate spheres. Sandford, for instance,
argues that since women have 'many trials . . . they . . .
need a sedative influence, and religion is the anodyne'
(Sandford 1831: 37). For Elizabeth Gaskell, however,
religion required woman as well as men to 'bear witness
to the truth': to act and to speak according to their own
convictions. These speaking, acting women, who have
been invisible to most Gaskell critics, are 'a species of
mole as yet not recognised. When they awaken from
among the dead, from among the words, from among
the laws . . .' (Cixous, in Marks and de Courtivron: 93).

Coda: Ideology as Doom

A text that was anathema to William and Elizabeth
Gaskell was that 'the sins of the fathers shall be visited
upon the children'. It conceives God as a vengeful, not
nurturing, Father and denies the child's right to self-
determination. Many of Elizabeth Gaskell's stories
reject the obligation of children to suffer in silence their
fathers' crimes. Parents, however, can visit their 'sins'
on children without committing crimes; the perpetuation of harmful ideologies is enough. To the Gaskells,
who saw reason and love as equally necessary for
humanity, the doctrine of 'separate spheres', which
assigned reason to men and love to women, was a denial
of full humanity to both. This harmful ideology is
attacked in all Elizabeth's work, but in two of her
supernatural tales it emerges as a curse passing from
generation to generation.

In *The Doom of the Griffiths* (1858), a Welsh family lives under a curse from the time of Glendower, that the family will end when the 'last male . . . shall slay the father' (*KI*; 238). The last son, Owen, alienated from his father, seeks love in a secret marriage with a low-born woman. In a discovery scene, the Squire kills Owen's baby, Owen kills his father, and Owen, his wife and her father are killed trying to escape. The doom is thus fulfilled. But the psychological crisis comes when the Squire, obsessed with family pride and patrilineal inheritance, confronts Owen, who, with his baby in his arms, is like an emblem of the 'nurturing male' of the working-class stories. The 'doom' of the Griffiths is one which every patriarchal family shares; the doom of perpetuating an ideal of manhood which allows men to be only half human. Owen rises against his father as John Barton against Carson, as representative of an unjust 'law' which prevents him from nurturing his child.

The Poor Clare is a more elaborate ghost story. Bridget, a servant, obsessively loves her beautiful daughter, Mary, who angers her mother by leaving home. Bridget, now reputed a witch, transfers her love to a spaniel dog, which is killed by a soldier, Gisborne. Bridget curses Gisborne with the threat that his best-beloved will 'become a terror and a loathing to all' (*K5*: 341). Gisborne, however, has seduced Mary and his best-beloved is their daughter, Lucy. Lucy is demure and virtuous but at puberty she begins to be accompanied by a monstrous double, 'a ghastly resemblance, complete in likeness . . . but with a loathsome demon soul looking out of the grey eyes, that were in turns mocking and voluptuous' (*K5*: 362).

The story is set in the early eighteenth century, and all the characters are Catholics or Puritans – both groups which practise repression of the flesh. Lucy's companion explains the haunting by claiming that ' "the sins of the fathers shall be visited upon the children" ' (K5: 363) – that is, Lucy is suffering for her father's sexual crime against her mother. In psychological terms, however, Lucy's double, which is seen, by everyone, makes visible the repressed sexuality of a whole society. The voluptuous demon is the paraxial image of its obsessive chastity (see Jackson 1981: 19 for the concept of the 'paraxial' in fantasy literature). The Mary that Bridget wanted at home, the demure Lucy approved by her father, are only half human, the product of an ideology which denies female autonomy. Bridget loves a child-Mary but rejects her as an adult, projecting her repressed fear of sexuality as a curse. Gisborne uses the sexual Mary, then 'kills' her like the spaniel and raises Lucy to be a child-woman in her turn, projecting his repressed desire as her voluptuous double. The characters within the story see Bridget's curse as responsible for the haunting and, as in *The Doom of the Griffiths*, we can see this curse as the passing on, from generation to generation, of a repressive ideology. Although Bridget and Gisborne seem at odds, they perpetuate the same tradition based on fears that women who are not treated as children will 'fall' into loathsome lechery.

Like much Victorian fantasy, *The Poor Clare* is not open-ended but offers an ideological resolution of the 'terrors' it has disclosed. This closure, however, is not a reinscription of the status quo but suggests an alternative social order. In the religious terms of the narrative, the curse is raised when Bridget, as an act of atonement, becomes a nun and devotes herself to public charity. In psychological terms, this represents a breach of her claustrophobic obsession with her daughter's chastity and a move towards adult involvement in the community. It is indicative of the complex and surprising meanings underlying Elizabeth Gaskell's explorations of 'motherhood' that Bridget's conventionally protective stance towards her biological daughter is expressed in a stepmother's or wicked fairy's curse, while her nurturing, fairy-godmother role is performed for strangers as one of a chaste sisterhood. As a 'Poor Clare' she relieves a war- and famine-stricken town, and the story ends with a moving scene in which the whole city unites in turn to relieve the Poor Clares. As women and old men, children and soldiers of both armies sweep through the streets with food for the starving nuns, we have an image of human nurturance, cooperation and communication which transcends both the 'masculine' world of war, which has killed Gisborne, and the enclosed 'feminine' world, which prompted Bridget's curse, whose '"roots . . . lie deeper than she knows. . . . The sins of the fathers are indeed visited upon the children"' (K5: 367).

Chapter Four

Mary Barton (1848)

A Manchester Love Story
(working title for *MB: L* 23)

Most critical accounts of *Mary Barton* begin with the *a priori* assumption that it falls into a clear category of fiction, the 'industrial' or 'social-problem' novel, which defines boths its proper subject-matter – class relations – and its proper orientation – political and economic. The 'faults' which most critics identify stem from this assumption. Firstly, they deplore the presence of 'extraneous factors' such as the love story and the murder plot (e.g. Lucas 1966: 162, 173–4), and secondly, they regret Elizabeth Gaskell's inadequate political grasp, taking her disclaimer that she knows 'nothing of Political Economy' (*MB*: 38) as a naïve acknowledgement of unfitness for the task she has undertaken. Yet her father's Blackwood's articles on 'The Political Economist' (Stevenson 1824–5) make it plain that the term 'economist' then meant 'only those who felt that the market mechanism was the best guide to economic development' (Fetter 1960: 90). Like her father, Elizabeth Gaskell dissociated herself from 'political economy' because she believed that humane ethical attitudes, rather than blind market forces, should govern social relationships (see also Hopkins 1931: 60).

Mary Barton develops a contrast between two ethical systems, that of the working class, based on caring and cooperation, and that of the middle class, based on ownership, authority and the law. The dichotomy is similar to the conventional gender-role division, and Elizabeth Gaskell has been criticised (e.g. Lucas 1966: 174) for trying to evade the question of class struggle with an inappropriate domestic ethic. She had, however, some justification for presenting the working class as observing a 'female ethic'. Like Wordsworth, she observed that one product of extreme poverty is mutual aid (*L* 12), and historians confirm that 'the workers . . . made thousands of tiny sacrifices daily in automatic response to the promptings of common humanity' (Cazamian [1903] 1973: 71). The result was a 'feminisation' of working-class men who performed from necessity the roles of child-care, sick-nursing and house-keeping; Angela Davis identifies the same effect in American slave families (Davis 1982: 18). Although these same men, in *Mary Barton*, take part in strikes, assaults and murders, Elizabeth Gaskell presents this aggressive action as an enforced and psychologically damaging expression of essentially nurturing motives. The single-minded masculinity of bourgeois men, on the other hand, finds appropriate articulation in their aggressive use of the forces of law and order. Rather than evading the question of class struggle, therefore, *Mary Barton* offers a *critique* of confrontational politics. Since aggression is the language of authority, the concept of class struggle as necessarily aggressive appears not as the will of the people but as a masculine, middle-class imposition.

Marxist critics like John Lucas see the love story and the murder plot as extraneous to *Mary Barton* because they see class confrontation as the only valid focus for the 'industrial theme'. Marxist feminists such as Nancy Chodorow, however, emphasise that individuals of both classes acquire the values which perpetuate or challenge capitalism through childhood socialisation, in which the status of the father is crucial. Although class struggle is most clearly seen in public confrontations, the family is the mechanism which reproduces class attitudes, and parent–child relationships, as worked out in the 'extraneous' sections of this novel, demonstrate how the personal becomes the political. If we approach the novel through the ethics of the family, therefore, we do not detract from its value as an exploration of class relations, but instead of seeing it as an 'industrial novel' flawed by political naïvety and superfluous sub-plots, we can see it as an attempt to understand the interaction of class and gender. In particular, its opposed class-based images of fatherhood prompt us to rethink the political concept of 'paternalism'.

Mary Barton begins with a chapter which stresses the nurturing role of working-class fathers. The rural family scene suggests the 'elementary feelings' of Wordsworth's 'low and rustic life' (Wordsworth [1801] 1963: 245), feelings which are shown to persist in the urban environment of the ham-and-egg tea. Eli Zaretsky confirms that 'proletarianisation' put a new emphasis on the family. Because the family 'was the only space that proletarians "owned"', it became the focus for personal fulfilment and the basis for social attitudes. 'The . . . Victorian ideology of the family as the repository of "human values" converged with the tradition of romantic revolt' (Zaretsky 1976:61). In Chapter 1, John Barton is shown partly as nurturing father and partly as political activist, as if mediating in his person the Latin meaning of 'proletarian' – 'he who has no wealth but his children' – and its meaning in capitalism – 'he who has no wealth but his labour' (O'Brien: 177). In every speech of his, throughout the book, which shows class antagonism, there is also mention of starving children. ' "If my child lies dying (as poor Tom lay, with his white wan lips quivering, for want of better food than I could give him), does the rich man bring the wine or broth that might save his life?" ' (*MB*: 45; see also 105, 126, 130, 143–4, 238, 251).

Barton has learned his nurturing role from his mother and identifies with her:

> When he was a little child, [he] had seen his mother hide her daily morsel to share it among her children, and . . . he, being the eldest, had told the noble lie, that 'he was not hungry, could not eat a bit more', in order to imitate his mother's bravery, and still the sharp wail of the younger infants. (p. 158)

Men who define themselves primarily in relation to the family at subsistence level partake of its 'female ethic', based on the survival of infants, which extends itself beyond the family in neighbourly help like that to the Davenports. 'Male morality', on the other hand, stresses transcendence of mere survival, and the middle-class father Carson is 'proud' of his son and daughter for being accomplished, well-dressed and well-mannered (*MB*: 107) – features which distinguish them from common humanity. The novel explicitly criticises Carson for not extending the same sort of paternal care to his workers that they show for one another (e.g. p. 458), and modern critics see this 'paternalism' as a weakness in Elizabeth Gaskell's political vision, confirming a relationship of inequality between the classes. The 'paternalism' practised by her working-class characters, however, is not only nurturing rather than authoritative, it is functional rather than innate. It can be temporary and *ad hoc*; John Barton feeds Mrs Davenport like a baby when she is sick, but later she becomes a nurse to old Alice. More importantly, it revolves with successive generations. Working-class 'parents' educate their children to take responsibility. Alice Wilson makes sure Will knows what a seafaring life is like, but then lets him go; when Margaret goes blind, her grandfather watches her down the street and, seeing that she can manage, lets her go (*MB*: 252). Moreover, they accept what Noddings calls the 'commitment of the cared-for to turn about and act as one-caring' (Noddings 1984: 95). In the course of the novel old Alice changes from foster-mother to foster-child and calls young Mary 'mother' (*MB*: 270); Jane Wilson calls her son Jem 'mammy' (p. 329); John Barton becomes 'childish' and is cared for by his daughter (p. 424). This pattern gives a new meaning to 'paternalism'. The middle-class concept of fatherhood, separated from motherhood and based on 'innate' authority, is indeed a cheat as a paradigm for class relations because the working class cannot acquire in turn the authority of the 'father' and 'grow up' into a class of owners. The caring, temporary and functional notion of fatherhood which Gaskell presents as characteristic of the working-class, on the other hand, easily passes into the principle of cooperation.

If *any* kind of parent–child paradigm seems offensive when applied to adults, we should remember that proletarianisation was a new phenomenon. Elizabeth

Gaskell's urban workers are the first or second generation of their kind. The codes of conduct evolved in a land-based environment are inappropriate to urban capitalism. The inadequacy of the workers to their new situation is rendered in all the social writings of the period in terms of inarticulacy and unsteadiness – characteristics of children (*infant* = unable to speak; see G. Beer, in Barker *et al.* 1978). But Gaskell also sees that the manufacturers have in a sense *created* this class of people, and have therefore a functional responsibility towards them. In Chapter 15, explaining the growth of class antagonism, Elizabeth Gaskell uses the image of Frankenstein and his monster (making the common mistake of giving the monster his creator's name):

> The actions of the uneducated seem to me typified in those of Frankenstein, that monster of many human qualities, ungifted with a soul. . . .
> The people rise up to life; they irritate us, they terrify us, and we become their enemies. Then, in the sorrowful moment of our triumphant power, their eyes gaze on us with a mute reproach. Why have we made them what they are; a powerful monster, yet without the inner means for peace and happiness? (*MB*: 219–20)

This image has only been noticed with embarrassment by critics of *Mary Barton* (e.g. Ganz 1969: 64), but feminist critics have seen the social significance of Mary Shelley's novel itself. Ellen Moers, for instance, sees it as a 'fantasy of the newborn as at once monstrous agent of destruction and piteous victim of parental abandonment' (Moers 1978: 97). Mary Daly says that 'Mary Shelley . . . unmasks the mentality of the technological "parent"' (Daly 1979: 70). Both claim that although the technocratic 'father' can *create* a 'child', he cannot nurture it. Frankenstein attempts to control his monster by physical restraint and by rules, which are ineffective, just as 'magistrates, and prisons, and severe punishments' (*MB*: 223) fail to restrain the Manchester strikers. Constraint by law alone is absurd, as if parents should 'make domestic rules for the pretty behaviour of children, without caring to know that those children had been kept for days without food' (p. 127). In a domestic economy of 'separate spheres' primary child-care is the province of the mother, but the Frankenstein model of the economy attempts to dispense with the maternal function. The monster is deprived, above all, of socialisation and is left to educate himself, obsessed with questions of origin, identity and purpose: '"Who was I? What was I? Whence did I come? What was my destination?"' (Shelley [1818] 1985: 170). In the same way, Barton is obsessed with 'the problems and mysteries of life . . . bewildered and lost, unhappy and suffering' (*MB*: 219).

Articulacy is the goal of the 'infant'. The monster confronts his maker with his speech on Mont Blanc; Barton takes the Chartist petition to Parliament. Speech promises participation in the symbolic order (see above, Ch. 1 (2v); it is a claim to be heard and replied to, accepted as 'adult' by the 'father'. Parental refusal of dialogue closes that path; the monster then 'learns' refusal, antagonism. The 'father' creates, instead of a son, an adversary. '"I ought to be thy Adam, but I am rather the fallen angel, whom thou drivest from joy for no misdeed"', says the monster (Shelley 1985: 142). Chapter 15 of *Mary Barton* makes it plain that the workers, as they move from the 'female ethic' of the family to the 'male morality' of the public world, 'learn' silence and resistance from the masters. At the end of the novel, John Barton, now repenting of the murder of Harry Carson, feels 'as if he could never lay bare the perverted reasoning which had made the performance of undoubted sin appear a duty' (*MB*: 436). But the ethic of revenge is part of the dominant ideology which Barton invokes in Chapter 1 when he cites the parable of Lazarus and Dives, gaining satisfaction from the punitive chasm set between them by Abraham/God. This invocation of revenge, or what Noddings calls 'the judgemental love of the harsh father' (Noddings 1984: 98), puts Barton on a level with Carson, who says, '"Let my trespasses be unforgiven, so that I may have vengeance for my son's murder"' (*MB*: 436). The 'murder plot', which critics see as an 'irrelevance' to the 'industrial theme' (e.g. Gill, *MB*: 22), is necessary to show that the avenging force which appears 'lawless' in the hands of the workers is in fact the ethic of the dominant ideology, supported by Church and law. The masters must refuse dialogue with the workers (p. 232) because to engage in speech with them would be to accept them as 'adults' and thus legitimise their access to the dominant 'language' of vengeance.

In *Mary Barton* the agents of the law prevent not crime but unauthorised speech; John Barton is struck by a London policeman when going to present the petition (p. 144); Esther is arrested ('a clear case of disorderly vagrancy', p. 170) when she tries to speak to John Barton, and a policeman threatens Jem when he tries to speak to Harry Carson (p. 230). After the murder, the police become nakedly the agents of revenge. Carson treats the superintendent as a personal servant and is prepared to buy 'justice' (p. 262). The phrase 'brought to justice' (p. 265) comes to have an ironic ring, and Gaskell emphasises the revenge motive:

True, his vengeance was sanctioned by law, but was it the less revenge?

Are we worshippers of Christ? or of Alecto? [one of the furies]

Oh! Orestes! you would have made a very tolerable Christian of the nineteenth century! (p. 266)

The mechanism of the law is implicated in Carson's 'craving thirst for blood. He would have fain been policeman, magistrate, accusing speaker, all; but most of all, the judge, rising with full sentence of death on his lips' (p. 274). Whereas William Gaskell uses the words 'vengeful and unjust' as equivalents (see above, Ch. 3 (4)), the trial scene shows that the law equates vengeance with justice. Carson is likened to a 'beast of prey' fearing that 'his victim [would be] taken from his hungry jaws' (p. 396), 'would slip through the fangs of justice' (p. 398). Mrs Wilson feels that 'the judge were some wild animal trying to rend thee from me' (p. 409). The narrative also exposes the adversarial system of law itself, in which lawyers are paid, not to discover the truth, but to attack one another (pp. 395, 397).

And all the time Carson is 'a noble-looking old man . . . so stern and inflexible, with such classical features' like 'some of the busts of Jupiter' (p. 384). Patriarchal power, symbolised by the 'father of the gods' and sanctioned by the institutions of law and order, is exposed as the primitive antagonism of wild animals.

The working-class 'female ethic' is endangered not only by the 'male morality' of adversarial justice but also by the middle-class concept of ornamental femininity. John Barton's hostility to Esther in Chapter 1 seems unreasonable when all he has against her is that she is '"fond of thinking herself"' a lady, and is fond of dress (pp. 43–4). Yet his sketch of the '"do-nothing lady, worrying shopmen all morning, and screeching at her pianny all afternoon, and going to bed without having done a good turn to any one of God's creatures but herself"' (p. 44), shows the incompatibility between decorative ladyhood and the useful, caring habits of the working class.

The cash-nexus economy forces men 'who have no wealth but their labour' into an antagonistic stance towards employers; for women the situation is complicated by the fact that not only their work but also their bodies have a cash value. Middle-class women play the marriage market; working-class women can take a risk – they may land a husband, as Mrs Carson did (p. 164), they may end up a cheap bargain, as Mary nearly does (p. 180), or as spoiled goods, like Esther (p. 168). What John Barton hates in all three categories is the fact that women are changed from useful, caring people into commodities incapable of doing anyone 'a good turn'. Reacting against the middle-class ideology of the 'pleasing female', he rightly focuses on dress. Ironically, he objects to factory work for Mary because the good wages would give her spare cash to spend on clothes (p. 43), and so she ends up working for a dressmaker, 'where the chief talk was of fashions, and dress, and . . . love and lovers' (p. 140) – the very ideology he wishes to avoid. Most critics see Mary's attention to dress and her ambition to marry Harry Carson as personal, moral failings, as 'vanity' and 'frivolity' (e.g. Ganz 1969: 70; Bergmann 1979: 30, 109). But ideologically, they represent a switch from the ethic of caring and cooperation to that of the commodity market. At the trial, Mr Carson sees Mary as 'the fatal Helen' (p. 388), a phrase which combines the concept of woman as a piece of disputed property, with the ethic of adversarial 'justice' – the dispute over Helen was settled by the Trojan War.

John Barton's encounter with Esther in Chapter 10

comes in the context of his growing hatred of the 'do-nothing' class which she seems to have joined, a class whose antagonism has changed him from 'Adam' to 'the fallen angel' (Shelley 1985: 142), and they meet in the 'darkness visible' of Milton's hell (*MB*: 168; *Paradise Lost* I, 63). Gilbert and Gubar note that Frankenstein, 'one of the key Romantic "readings" of *Paradise Lost* . . . is most especially the story of hell' (Gilbert and Gubar 1979: 221). Barton and Esther are here both 'fallen' from the 'Eden of innocence' (*MB*: 292), the 'elementary feelings' of 'low and rustic life', into the divisive ideology of separate spheres. Both might have said, with Anne Finch, ' "How are we fal'n, fal'n by mistaken rules" ' (quoted in Gilbert and Gubar 1979: 219); Esther has become a sexual commodity, and John an avenger, 'a sort of accusing angel' (*MB*: 292). It is appropriate, therefore, that for the only time in the novel he behaves like a middle-class man, and asserts superiority over a woman. Esther is left sobbing, ' "He would not listen to me . . . " ' (p. 170), a poignant echo of John's own earlier words, ' "we mun speak to our God to hear us, for man will not hearken . . . " ' (p. 141).

Esther's attempts at speech, however, follow rather than precede her 'fall', and are born of a 'monomaniacal' compulsion like the Ancient Mariner's, to tell her ghastly tale with its moral of love (p. 207). When she tries to speak to Jem in Chapter 14, he initially shrugs her off, in a gesture that becomes a *leit-motif* for the novel (p. 208; see pp. 144, 169, 228). But the 'spell' of Mary's name 'was as potent as that of the Mariner's glittering eye. "He listened like a three-year child" ' (p. 208). Jem is thus the wedding-guest, who may learn the 'moral' without himself having to suffer the purgatorial journey.

When Esther visits Mary in Chapter 21, she feels 'as if

some holy spell would prevent her (even as the unholy Lady Geraldine was prevented, in the abode of Christabel) from crossing the threshold of that home of her early innocence' (p. 293). Christabel's 'holy' mother and the usurping Geraldine in Coleridge's poem function as ideological 'doubles' like the double Lucy in *The Poor Clare* (see above, Ch. 3 (Coda)). In *Mary Barton* also, the physical likeness of the fallen Esther and her virtuous sister seems ironically to point their moral divergence. Unexpectedly, however, no 'holy spell' prevents Esther from speaking to Mary. In a remarkable apotheosis at the end of Chapter 20 – recalling the moon/mother scene in Chapter 27 of *Jane Eyre*, which Elizabeth Gaskell had not yet read (*L* 25a) – Esther functions as the agent of divine/maternal influence. 'There, against the moonlight, stood a form, so closely resembling her dead mother, that Mary never doubted the identity, but exclaim[ed] (as if she were a terrified child, secure of safety when near the protecting care of its parent) "Oh! mother! mother! You are come at last!"' (p. 287). As so often in Elizabeth Gaskell's work, the parental impulse is more important than parental identity. In the moment of crisis, Esther functions as a mother for Mary, and the madonna/magdalen double is united.

Esther's maternal message, the fruit of her 'fallen' experience, is the opposite of the gentlewoman's 'duty', to 'suffer and be still'. By bringing Mary the valentine/ gun-wadding, she raises her from the posture of prostrate suffering (p. 285) to 'the necessity for exertion' (p. 301).

Mary's whole story is a chiasmic change from being the silent object of others' contemplation to a speaking subject unconscious of her appearance. In the early chapters her concern even with other people who are to appear in public is with their clothes (pp. 128-9, 136). Absorbed in the gossip of the dress-shop, she doesn't hear of the failure of the petition (p. 141), and when her father and Job Legh discuss it, she falls asleep. The over-pretty description of her 'sleeping soundly as any infant' (p. 153), presents her as a 'picture' and as a baby. By the time of the trial, however, she shrugs off Sally, who wants to know what she will wear (p. 336), and appears with 'the rich treasure of her golden hair, stuffed away in masses under her little bonnet-cap' (p. 389). On the other hand, her determination to speak brings 'dignity, self-reliance, and purpose' (p. 318); 'she began to take confidence, and to have faith in her own powers' (p. 330).

Ironically, although Esther and Jem, and indirectly her father, are all concerned to 'save' Mary from Harry Carson, she does not need 'saving' and deals with him competently herself on the basis of the ethics learned in her childhood (pp. 183-4; cf. Noddings 1984: 1). Her real test comes with her discovery that her father is a murderer, which casts doubt not only on his personal worth but also on the system of values which he represented. The act 'seemed to separate him into two persons, - one, the father who had dandled her on his knee, and loved her all her life long; the other, the assassin, the cause of her trouble and woe' (p. 413). Like Esther in the 'darkness visible', John has become a 'phantom likeness of John Barton; himself, yet not himself' (p. 414).

The effect on Mary is to make her doubt her own identity and values. Chapter 19 is prefaced with a quotation from Coleridge's 'The Pains of Sleep', stressing moral confusion: 'I could not know,/ Whether I suffered or I did,/ For all seemed guilt, remorse, or woe' (p. 267); and in Chapter 20 she asks, 'Was it not she who had led him to the pit into which he had fallen?' (p. 285).

The valentine/gun-wadding symbolises the involution of innocence with guilt. John Barton's act of murder is motivated by love as 'innocent' as Samuel Bamford's verses, 'God help the poor', or Jem's message of love for Mary, both of which are inscribed on the valentine which 'innocently' facilitates the fatal shot. Yet the 'guilty' act must somehow be separated from the 'innocent' motive. Like Elizabeth Gaskell's ghost stories, John Barton's phantom 'double' is best seen in terms of conflicting ideologies (see above, Ch. 3 Coda). Ideologies do not provide motives (such as parental love), but they provide the means by which these primary impulses can 'speak'. John Barton, having failed to speak 'openly, and clearly, as appealing to reasonable men' (p. 232), 'falls' into the middle-class 'language' of violence. Mary's sense of her father's 'fall' is suggested by the quotation at the head of Chapter 22, from Keat's *Hyperion*, where Thea approaches the old god Saturn, king of the Titans, defeated in his war with Jupiter. Bereft of paternal guidance, she has a 'conviction of how much rested upon her unassisted and friendless self, alone with her terrible knowledge' (p. 303). In order to act and speak, she draws 'a black veil . . . over her father's past, present and future life' (p. 324) and focuses her mind on Jem, the 'wedding-guest' who has inherited both Esther's 'moral' and the lessons of the unfallen fathers of Chapter 1. In this way, she is able to speak from an alternative ethic to the adversarial system. Although the legal summons requires her '"to bear witness again[st] Jem Wilson"' (p. 314), she finds a way 'to bear witness to the truth'; to prove Jem innocent without accusing anyone; to seek remedy rather than revenge; in Carol Gilligan's terms, she favours 'that resolution in which no one is hurt' (Gilligan 1977: 515). The novel thus suggests that in the class war, also, it is unnecessary to accuse. Everyone has an 'innocent motive'; what is in question is whether the motives will 'speak' in the mode of remedial or adversarial justice.

Mary's clarity on behalf of Jem is undermined by the moral chaos behind the 'veil' hiding her father's fall. Since it is through the father that adults acquire access to language, the father's 'fall' threatens the child with inarticulacy. As soon as the immediate object of finding Will is achieved, Mary finds that she has no secure ethical base; 'her very words seemed not her own, and beyond her power of control' (*MB:* 359). Her moral danger is indicated when, at the trial, she is likened to Beatrice Cenci (p. 389), who turned her father's violent methods against himself. Unlike Beatrice, Mary uses her brief public power not to kill her father but to affirm her love for Jem, but Jem's safety cannot validate her father's crime. Exhausted by the effort of distinguishing truth and silence from falsehood (p. 394), unable either to accept or reject her 'double' father, she refuses consciousness. In delirium, 'sight and hearing were no longer channels of information to that poor distracted brain' (p. 401).

The *impasse* is resolved by a process which reads like a curious pre-vision of Chodorow's psychoanalytic insight that social change must begin with the imprinting on infantile minds of maternal care from men (see above, Ch. 1 (2vi)). Mary, her mind reduced by trauma to 'the tender state of a lately born infant's' (*MB:* 415), recognises Jem 'as a baby does when it sees its mother tending its little cot' (p. 416). In this strange parody of a mother–child dyad, Mary's avenging father is an 'awful forbidden ground of discourse (p. 419) until, strengthened by Jem's 'maternal' care, she is able to see not his 'savage . . . wayward violence' (pp. 420-1) but his 'smitten helplessness' (p. 422). Assuming adult responsibility, Mary now becomes mother to her own father, who speaks 'in a weak, high, childish voice' (p. 424). Chapters 33 to 36 pass in a dizzying permutation of mother–child relationships. Even the patriarchal Carson is prompted to reread the Bible in the spirit of a 'little child' (p. 440); and his support of the dying Barton is like that of the Madonna in Michelangelo's *Pietà* (p. 442). The novel thus urgently seeks to redress what Noddings identifies as a major lack in our culture: 'ethics has been discussed largely in the language of the father: in principles and propositions. . . . The mother's voice has been silent . . . the memory of caring and being cared for, which I shall argue form the foundation of ethical response, have not received attention except as outcomes of ethical behaviour' (Noddings 1984: 1). It is ironic, therefore, that the parental theme has been invisible to critics of *Mary Barton*, who understandably find its message somewhat thin – 'grotesquely inadequate' according to Lucas (1966: 174), while Stephen Gill complains that 'the diagram at the end of Barton dying in Carson's arms appears to say something about conflict and brotherhood, when in fact it has grown out of a progressive simplification of the issues with which the novel confronted us at its outset' (*MB*: 27; cf. Ganz 1969: 80). The novel may not say much about brotherhood, but it says a great deal about fatherhood.

If we read *Mary Barton* as a novel about fatherhood – a relationship rather than a person – we can to some extent escape the debate about who is the central character. We should also be able to see, however, why Elizabeth Gaskell conceived John Barton as her 'tragic . . . "hero"' (*L* 39). As a working-class father, male proponent of a 'female ethic', he suffers in his person that disjunction of private and public values which was the nineteenth century's most traumatic schism. As father to his family, he is his mother's son – feeding the children comes first. As a 'child' in the public world, however, he encounters only the patriarch Carson, who doesn't '"pretend to know the names"' of his workers (*MB*: 109). The 'piteous victim of parental abandonment' (Moers 1978: 97), he receives neither help nor instruction; '"no one learned me, and no one told me"' (*MB*: 440). In the context of an aggressive individualism whose motto is '"Stand up for thy rights"'', the official altruism of the New Testament seems '"a sham put upon . . . women"' (p. 440), yet it still comes '"natural to love folk"'. Barton's attempts at self-education founder in this ideological rift between a language in which 'father' = 'love' and one in which 'father' = 'law', a rift which tears him '"in two"' (p. 441). Sanity and the social contract alike depend on shared meanings: '"you'd never believe black was black . . . when you saw all about you acting as if black was white" ' (p. 440). The incomprehensibly double meaning of fatherhood reduces him progressively to 'silence' (pp. 141, 162), 'incipient madness' (p. 219) and a ghoulish 'double' existence (p. 413).

As a critique of fatherhood, *Mary Barton* needs its 'irrelevant' sub-plots. The 'murder plot' demonstrates how the dominant ideology sanctions vengeance, not succour, as the expression of paternal 'care', and the 'romance plot' offers Jem as the worker/father of the future, when workers will be 'educated . . . not mere machines of ignorant men' (p. 460). Jem the inventor is the real source of technological progress, 'The Modern Prometheus' instead of 'Frankenstein's monster', but he is also a 'family man', whose marriage is contracted in an ambience almost absurdly maternal, with everyone acting as mother to everyone else, and whose little son greets him at the end with 'a crow of delight' (p. 465). Yet the family grouping at the end curiously effaces Mary.

Under necessity, she reasoned, spoke and acted in the public world, protecting her father and rescuing Jem, but her role ends with this enablement of her menfolk. Jem, his roots nourished by the 'female ethic', blossoms in the world of technology, but Mary's life is as private as her mother's.

Mary Barton thus embodies an irony. Born of its author's grief as a mother at the death of her infant son (*L* 25a), and of her care as a woman for the sufferings of her neighbours, its impulse is profoundly maternal. Yet its most notable absence is Mary's mother, whose 'female ethic' is the standard from which John and Esther fall, but whose domestic field of action is too small for the crusading message Elizabeth Gaskell wishes to spread. The 'mother's voice' speaks in the public world only through men – not only the male characters of the novel but also the male writers whose 'language' defines its parameters.

The domestic ending, which irritates socialists and feminists alike, is generally read as a peculiarly feminine lapse – a case of 'Mrs Gaskell' naïvely or carelessly reverting from radical politics to cosy romance. Yet it is more likely to derive from the masculine tradition of Romantic revolt which she uses to 'authorise' her radical text. For the novel is densely haunted by literary 'fathers': her own father's essays on political economy; her husband's lectures on 'The Poets and Poetry of Humble Life'; Wordsworth's reverence for the poor who are ' "the fathers . . . [of] small blessings" ' (*L* 12); the New Testament, which promises maternal care from the suffering son of a loving father; the People's Charter, in which women are invisible; Carlyle, who on the title-page addresses the novelist as 'worthy brother'; the Romantic poets of the chapter-mottoes – Goethe, Coleridge, Burns, Crabbe, Keats, Southey, Shelley,

Byron; *Frankenstein*, another woman's text with a notably absent mother, haunted by Godwin, Shelley and Byron (see Rubinstein 1976); and ultimately, though there is no explicit reference, Rousseau, whose influence permeated the Romantic movement and early Utopian socialism. Rousseau's strength in his wish to 'bring to public life sympathy, love, affection and the supportive solidarity of family relationships'. His now notorious weakness is to exclude women. His ideal is a 'Brotherhood' of man working for the public good, while women 'choose' to fertilise 'its enigmatic roots in the private realm' (O'Brien 1981: 96–7).

This is the programme which indirectly determines the ending of *Mary Barton*. Its political naïvety is thus not that of female incompetence but of the male-stream tradition of pre-Marxist revolt. But as a dutiful daughter of Romanticism, Elizabeth Gaskell unwittingly betrays her maternal text, entrusting her female ethic to a 'Brotherhood' defined by its difference from women.

Only in this first novel, in fact, does she put faith in an ideal father. From *North and South* she confronts the fact that men of all classes are governed, in the public sphere, by a masculine code which precludes 'feminine' tenderness.

Chapter Five

Cranford (1851)

In the first place, Cranford is in possession of the Amazons.

(C: 39)

Cranford, always the most popular of Elizabeth Gaskell's novels, reprinted more than once a year since its first publication, has until recently seemed unproblematically charming. The women's movement, however, has produced some startling rereadings. Whereas Cecil, for instance, saw Miss Matty as a 'wistful figure' of 'fragile, flower-like grace' (Cecil 1934: 220), Nina Auerbach sees her as a biblical avenger with a 'savage mission' (Auerbach 1978: 83). The ground for this divergence lies in the novel's opening sentence, quoted above. To what extent is it ironic? Since the legendary Amazons were warriors and the ladies of Cranford are 'gentle, kind, affectionate and feminine', it seems entirely so (Keating, C: 16). Are there ways, however, in which the ladies of Cranford are like Amazons? As warriors? As sexually mutilated? As hostile to men? As a community of

87

women? And, if these parallels can be sustained, does the novel present them as desirable?

Critics who take the Amazonian reference seriously either, like Dodsworth, focus on Cranford's militant hostility to men, epitomised by Miss Deborah Jenkyns, or, like Tarratt, Wolfe and Auerbach, focus on the caring community of women, epitomised by Miss Matty. Both approaches assume that Cranford, as a society of widows and spinsters, is an anomalous exception to Victorian society at large. I shall argue, however, that both the hostility and the community of Cranford are effects of the orthodox doctrine of separate spheres, and thus not triumphs over patriarchy but results of marginalisation. The positive movement of the novel comes not from female separatism but from women and men who work and care for children.

Martin Dodsworth sees Miss Jenkyns as a feminist whose misguided hostility to men has to be expiated by the Cranford community after her death. But both Tarratt and Wolfe rightly argue that the novel criticises Miss Jenkyns not for 'aggressive feminism' but for perpetuating the '"strict code of gentility"' which governed Cranford 'whilst Parson Jenkyns [was] still a dominating patriarch' (Tarratt 1968: 155, 158). 'Instead of being a leader in the cause of feminine superiority . . . Deborah existed simply as a shadow of . . . her father' (Wolfe 1968: 163). Miss Matty confirms this: '"She was such a daughter to my father, as I think there never was before, or since. His eyes failed him, and she read book after book, and wrote, and copied, and was always at his service in any parish business"' (C: 102). This picture of Deborah reading and writing for her blind father reveals her as one of 'Milton's daughters' (Gilbert and Gubar 1979: 189), whose education was merely instrumental to their father's needs. Like Athena, the goddess of wisdom who was 'born' from the head of Zeus, Deborah 'remained childless and . . . seemed to have no memory of her . . . female origins' (Chesler 1974: xv–xvi). Athena is a lapsed Amazon, 'a virgin-warrior who helps men' (p. 26), just as, in the Bible, Deborah the Hebrew prophetess inspires men to feats of arms (Judges 4–5). The novel's repeated references to Dr Johnson should be seen in this context. Miss Jenkyns believes that by adopting Johnson's 'voice' she can acquire his authority, but the 'me too' feminist is never accepted as equal by those who hold power. '"Dr Johnson's style is a model for young beginners"', she says, '"My father recommended it to me when I began to write letters"' (C: 48). But *The New Female Instructor* quotes Johnson's letters *verbatim* as models in a chapter which also warns women not to attempt subjects 'in which their want of knowledge would expose them to ridicule' (NFI: 23). And Johnson, though he surrounded himself with intelligent women, would have laughed at a Hebrew prophetess. He compared women preachers with dancing dogs: 'one marvels not at how well it is done, but that it is done at all' (Ozick, in Gornick and Moran 1971: 435).

Miss Jenkyns is thus a sad paradox. Though apparently 'strong-minded' and 'superior' (C: 51), she has assimilated the conditions of her own subordination. Her intellect and her 'strict code of gentility' (p. 109) have become a means by which the dead father rules the community of women. The social rules announced in Chapter 1 'with all the solemnity with which the old Manx laws were read once a year on the Tinwald Mount' (p. 40) seem at first to codify female autonomy, but in fact they maintain male-orientated kinship structures. Mrs Jamieson, Miss Jenkyns' successor as social arbiter, decides a point of protocol as follows: 'whereas a married woman takes her husband's rank by the strict laws of precedence, an unmarried woman retains the station her father occupied' (p. 199). Women are thus defined not by who they are but by who they belong to.

Genteel as the code appears, moreover, it is belligerently maintained. The Rev. Jenkyns gives his son a public flogging for insubordination (p. 96). Miss Jenkyns sees Captain Brown's denigration of Johnson as 'a challenge' (p. 47) and gives a 'finishing blow or two' to her defence (p. 48). Mrs Jamieson conducts a one-sided 'feud' with Lady Glenmire, supported by 'Mr Mulliner, like a faithful clansman' (p. 205) – the Scottish clans are an extreme example of adversarial government in which disputes are settled by warfare. This belligerence is adopted by Cranford's Amazons as the 'language' of dominance, but they use it to defend a code which defines them as 'relative creatures'.

Dodsworth is thus wrong to take Miss Jenkyns as the feminist focus of the novel. Feminist critics emphasise Cranford's supportive female relationships, and especially Miss Matty, who in many ways epitomises what Noddings calls a feminine ethic. She opposes the competitive commercialism of Drumble, for instance. When the bank fails, her response is not self-interest but 'common honesty' towards the holders of bank-notes (p. 177) and 'sympathy' for the bank directors, to whom, in accordance with Noddings's ethic, she attributes the best of motives (p. 195; Noddings 1984: 123). She will not start her tea business without making sure that it will not injure the general grocer. The businessman, Mr Smith, '"wondered how tradespeople were to get on if there was to be a continual consulting of each other's interest, which would put a stop to all competition directly"' (C: 200). The answer, as Noddings would hope, is that 'her unselfishness and simple sense of justice called out the same good qualities in others' (p. 201).

Matty is also opposed to 'the strict code of gentility' wherever it threatens personal relationships. She is Peter's confidante in his practical jokes (p. 94) and likens her angry father to King Ahauserus (p. 97). She finds a humane reason to visit Mrs Fitz-Adam (p. 109) and disassociates herself from Mrs Jamieson's exclusiveness (pp. 116, 199). Although she is timid at the thought of a burglar (pp. 147-8), she faces her bankruptcy with quiet courage (p. 179). Above all, she is loving – a characteristic demonstrated, as so often in Elizabeth Gaskell's stories, by a fondness for nursing babies (pp. 158, 212). When she loses her money, her example calls out the best in all her friends, and in the meeting of ladies which creates a trust fund for her support, we see the idea of a female community in a very positive light (p. 191). For these reasons Patricia Wolfe makes Miss Matty her heroine, and Nina Auerbach claims that 'in the verbal and commercial battle of nineteenth-century England, the cooperative female community defeat the warrior world that proclaims itself the real one' (Auerbach 1978: 87).

I would argue, however, that although the 'cooperative female community' is admirable, it is not triumphant. All it can do is to make the best of the little space allowed it. We do no service to women by ignoring the extent to which Miss Matty and the others have been diminished as human beings by the constraints of femininity. Matty herself is feeble and inactive, preferring darkness and often falling asleep (C: 84). Though barely 50, she has the senile fragility born of an eventless life. Even in the crisis of her bankruptcy, she 'would timidly have preferred a little more privation to any exertion' (p. 197). This stasis also characterises Mrs Jamieson, who exhibits 'the wearied manner of the Scandinavian prophetess, – "Leave me, leave me to repose"' (pp. 68-9).

Mrs Jamieson is 'fat and inert' (p. 64) and frequently falls asleep (pp. 112, 134). Miss Matty falls asleep while Mr Holbrook reads a poem, just as the 'infants' Mary Barton and Sylvia Robson do (*MB*: 153; *SL*: 95), and is startled by the decisive actions of men – by Peter's flight and Holbrook's journey to Paris. The mere turning of the earth makes her feel 'so tired and dizzy whenever she thought about it' (*C*: 127). She is intimidated by male control of language, so that 'words that she would spell quite correctly in her letters to me, became perfect enigmas when she wrote to my father' (p. 186). As 'we did not read much, or walk much' (p. 64) in Cranford, much ingenuity is needed to find topics of conversation (p. 49). The proliferation of specialised names of fabrics – 'mousseline-de-laine', 'sarsenet' (p. 70), 'Padu-asoy' (p. 86), 'bombazine' (p. 108) – reflects that narrowing preoccupation with dress deplored by Mary Wollstonecraft (*W*: 83).

The ignorance of all the Cranford ladies, which appears merely comic in Chapter 1 (*C*: 39), becomes baffling when Mary Smith tries to get information about Peter's whereabouts through a maze of loosely associated ideas involving the Great Lama of Thibet, the veiled prophet in Lalla Rookh, Rowlands' Kalydor, through llamas to Peruvian bonds and joint-stock banks:

> In vain I put in 'When was it – in what year was it that you heard that Mr Peter was the Great Lama?' They only joined issue to dispute whether llamas were carnivorous animals or not; in which dispute they were not quite on fair grounds, as Mrs Forrester . . . acknowledged that she always confused carnivorous and graminivorous together, just as she did horizontal and perpendicular; but then she apologized for it very prettily, by saying that in her day the

only use people made of four-syllabled words was to teach
how they should be spelt. (pp. 163–46)

When Miss Matty is faced with penury, her ignorance
becomes poignant:

> I thought of all the things by which a woman, past middle
> age, and with the education common to ladies fifty years
> ago, could earn or add to a living, without materially losing
> caste; but at length I put even this last chance to one side,
> and wondered what in the world Miss Matty could do.
> (p. 184)

In spite of her dignity and courage and her loving nature,
Miss Matty is not a heroine in the sense of being a model
for admiration. She is rather a victim of the nineteenth
century's systematic infantilisation of women.

Although the opening sentence of Cranford seems to
set a gulf between the Cranford Amazons and more
'normal' Victorian wives and mothers, the sentences
following reveal Cranford as only an extreme version of
'separate spheres':

> If a married couple come to settle in the town, somehow the
> gentleman disappears; he is either fairly frightened to death
> by being the only man in the Cranford evening parties, or
> he is accounted for by being with his regiment, his ship, or
> closely engaged in business all the week in the great
> neighbouring commercial town of Drumble. (p. 39)

The list of masculine occupations is typical, not just of
Cranford, but of Victorian England in general. There is
plenty of evidence that middle-class men and women did
lead severely segregated lives, before, during and after
marriage. Carrol Smith-Rosenberg, in a study of

women's friendships in nineteenth-century America, reports that:

> while hostility and criticism of other women were so rare as to seem almost tabooed, young women permitted themselves to express a great deal of hostility toward peer-group men. When unacceptable suitors appeared, girls might even band together to harass them . . . men appear as an other or out group. . . . With marriage both women and men had to adjust to life with a person who was, in essence, a member of an alien group. (Smith-Rosenberg 1975: 20, 28)

Intense female friendships, and 'emotional stiffness and distance' towards men, co-existed with a pattern of life orientated towards courtship and marriage. In this context, we can see that the 'women's community' of Cranford is in no sense an alternative culture to that of the dominant Victorian male but rather a supportive sub-culture delimited by the dominant group.

The female support networks described by Smith-Rosenberg are, however, more dynamic than Cranford's, because they are not just enclosed circles; their 'ethic of caring' extends onwards in time through generational ties, and outwards in space through contact with 'proximate strangers' (Noddings 1984: 46–7). Cranford's 'strict code of gentility' has the effect of closing the circle and cutting chains of connection: 'as Miss Pole observed, "As most of the ladies of good family in Cranford were elderly spinsters, or widows without children, if we did not relax a little . . . by-and-by we should have no society at all"' (C: 109). Auerbach reads *Cranford* as a triumph of the principle of friendship as opposed to kinship: 'destitute of the props and dimensions of the Victorian woman's life, the relationships of daughter, mother, and wife, Matty is restored as she presides over an organic community rooted in the past

and containing the future' (Auerbach 1978: 89). There
is, however, a sleight-of-hand in this argument, since
the community only 'contains the future' in the shape of
other people's children. The chains of connection come
through working women, children and 'proximate
strangers'. Signor Brunoni's magic and his need for
nursing, Signora Brunoni's tale of her journey on foot to
save her child (C: 160-1), Martha's outspoken love for
Jem Hearn, her quick thinking in the financial crisis, her
confinement and her baby, Lady Glenmire's 'sharp,
stirring ways' and ungenteel marriage – these are the
events which bring Cranford alive.

Most of the men in the novel also expand the inner
circle by creating generational or geographical links.
Apart from Parson Jenkyns and Mr Smith, who
represent different versions of 'masculine omnipotence'
(Auerbach 1978: 85), all the men in *Cranford* violate the
'code of gentility' (one aspect of which is to perpetuate
the sexes as 'alien groups') and speak in the female
language of care and support. Mr Hoggins, the surgeon,
only 'accepted' by virtue of his profession, is, like
Gaskell's other doctors, a nurturing presence. Captain
Brown, who violates the code by speaking of his poverty
(C: 42), also nurses his sick daughter (p. 46), helps a poor
woman carry home her dinner (p. 49) and dies saving
a child's life (p. 55). Mr Holbrook, who stubbornly
prefers 'yeoman' to 'esquire' and eats his peas with a
knife, has the sensitivity to nature and literature which
Elizabeth Gaskell associates with elementary human
feelings (p. 69).

Above all, Peter Jenkyns, though born of the Rectory,
serves to undermine its values, mocking his father and
Deborah. His dressing up as Deborah with a baby is
motivated not by a malicious wish to slander her virtue,
but by a sense that Deborah with a baby was the most

incongruous and therefore funny thing that he could think of. Unerringly, he exposes the sterile aspect of Amazonian superiority: 'Perfection is terrible, it cannot have children' (Plath, 1965: 74-5). He is '"like dear Captain Brown in always being ready to help any old person or a child"' (C: 94) and instead of killing the natives of Burma he cures them (p. 209). Whereas 'Deborah and her father shaped Cranford's social code, Matty and her mother [shaped] its moral and ethical standards' (Wolfe 1968: 172-3), and in this dichotomy, Peter stands with Matty and their mother in opposition to paternal law (p. 175).

Peter, however, has important advantages over Miss Matty and the other ladies. As a man and a traveller he is self-reliant, decisive, has a store of information and a flexible imagination. When he arrives in Cranford, the languge of Dr Johnson and the 'strict code' is fading and the ladies' minds have been exercised by genuine events – Miss Matty's ruin and Lady Glenmire' wedding. Peter offers them a new language. He tells 'stories . . . like Baron Munchausen's (p. 208), 'more wonderful stories than Sinbad the Sailor; and, as Miss Pole said, was quite as good as an Arabian Night any evening' (p. 211). 'Scheherezade', the wonderful storyteller of *The Arabian Nights*, was a Dickens's name for Elizabeth Gaskell, and *Cranford* establishes Dickens himself, the spell-binding author of *The Pickwick Papers*, as the antithesis of Dr Johnson. Dickens, Gaskell and Peter Jenkyns thus represent a new, fertile, Romantic mode of speech which 'astonishingly stir[s] up' the 'quiet lives' of the Cranford ladies (p. 211). The creative possibilities of this mode, shown in Peter's tale of shooting a cherubim (p. 217), contrast with the fixed truths of Dr Johnson and Miss Jenkyns, which claim to cover all eventualities, though they 'survey mankind from China to Peru'. Whereas

Rasselas helps Helen Burns in *Jane Eyre* (Ch. 5) to maintain quietist resignation, Peter's fantastic tales keep even Mrs Jamieson 'roused and animated' (C: 216) and open to dialogue even with the despised Mrs Hoggins.

In place of the rules and antagonisms of the dead father, Peter offers the remedial powers of speech as exploration and dialogue, powers denied to the ladies of Cranford by 'the education common to ladies fifty years ago' (p. 184). The Cranford Amazons do not 'triumph', as Wolfe and Auerbach claim, because they remain a muted group. But Peter's prominence does not prove, as Dodsworth claims, that they are defeated. Always linked with the maternal principle, Peter has escaped the genteel socialisation which would have put him in an 'alien group'. The brother–sister bond, based on shared memories of maternal care and childhood intimacy (p. 208), diminishes sex-antagonism. Peter aims not to silence Matty but to lend her his voice.

The flaw in his position is revealed in the painful episode in the last chapter where Peter makes a joke of Matty's failed engagement to Mr Holbrook. The clue to his crass insensitivity, so inconsistent with his general warmth of sympathy, lies in the detail of his language. His mental 'model' of the situation is one in which 'little Matty' is emotionally and sexually inert; he recognises that Holbrook '"cared for"' Matty, but not the reverse; he expects him to ' "carry [her] off" ' (p. 213). The only activity he conceives as possible for Matty is the purely economic one of husband-hunting; she must have ' "played [her] cards badly"' and ' "wanted [her] brother to be a good go-between"'. As a (failed) economic manoeuvre, Matty's 'play' for Holbrook seems fair game for a joke; her deeper needs are simply invisible to him. This blindness is not idiosyncratic but common to an ideology in which to impute sexuality to a woman is an insult. Fathers enforced their daughters' asexuality with rules, but mothers also endorsed it by their silence.

We are told that Parson Jenkyns and Deborah disapproved of Matty's engagement; her mother remains silent (p. 69). It is likely, however, that this mother/daughter silence would cover an unspoken sympathy, born of a common oppression which Peter does not share. Whereas a woman's silent denial of sexual motive covers a troubling consciousness of its existence, Peter, like Victorian medical experts (cf. Greg 1850: 457; Trudgill 1976: 56), takes silence as proof of absence. His loud masculine voice, useful in propagating 'female' warmth and harmony, here takes as 'given' a female lack which only women know to be a fiction.

This jarring breach in the Pickwickian geniality of the closing chapters is a seed of repressed anger about the infantile status of women which is most finely explored in *Cousin Phillis*. Just as Peter sees his 50-year-old sister as 'little Matty', so most of Elizabeth Gaskell's otherwise admirable men consign their sisters, wives and daughters to perpetual childhood. Cynthia Ozick argues that 'The Demise of the Dancing Dog' will occur in a future whose voice is neither a man's nor a woman's, but 'two voices' (in Gornick and Moran 1971: 450). Like *Mary Barton*, however, most of *Cranford* suggests that sympathetic men can 'speak for' women's values in the public world. But the bleak lapse in the last chapter, where Peter so blithely fails to 'give voice' to Matty's feeling, points to a problem which the most 'maternal' of Victorian men was unlikely to perceive. While *Mary Barton* presents the tragic self-division of the 'maternal man' as that between public and private values, *Cranford* hints that the schism is rooted in the family itself, where men may adopt women's values but deny their voices in denying their persons.

Chapter Six

Ruth (1853)

Yet – hear my protest! Why should she die?
(Charlotte Brontë to Elizabeth Gaskell,
1852, quoted in Gérin 1976: 132)

Ruth, with its difficult focus on the 'fallen woman', has prompted most of its readers to 'protest' in one way or another and has never been a popular book. Knowing that she was stirring a hornets' nest, Elizabeth Gaskell was unusually anxious during its composition and unusually sensitive to criticism (*L* 150). Some of her contemporaries protested against her even broaching an '"unfit subject for fiction"'. The book was banned, burned and denounced from the pulpit, making her feel like 'St Sebastian tied to a tree to be shot at with arrows' (*L* 148).

Readers like Charlotte Brontë, Elizabeth Barrett Browning and W.R. Greg, on the other hand, applauded *Ruth*'s challenge to the assumption that a woman's sexual 'fall' is 'the leper-sin' from which 'all stand aloof dreading to be counted unclean' (*MB*: 207), but protested at its failure of courage and consistency. Before her 'fall', they argued, Ruth is so innocent that she has nothing to repent of; afterwards, her penitence is insisted on. Modern readers see this inconsistency as an artistic rather than a moral failure. Ruth's 'extreme innocence and ignorance' are found unconvincing, a weak 'concession to the novel convention' (Fryckstedt 1982: 164), while 'the deep religiosity of ... tone is too emphatic for modern taste' (Gérin 1976: 130–1).

Ruth is indeed a problematic novel, flawed by 'fundamental contradictions' (Basch 1974: 249), which produce gaps, false leads and inconsistencies in the narrative surface. I shall argue, however, that these rifts and flaws are not simple (and uninteresting) failures of 'artistic unity', but significant failures of ideological coherence. The disruptive factor is female sexuality, which cannot be acknowledged in the ideological surface of the novel, but is repressed, emerging as a sub-text of imagery and dreams.

Elizabeth Gaskell's apprehension at tackling an 'improper' subject produced various kinds of overstatement – a prominent guilt-and-redemption structure, frequent biblical quotation and an excessively innocent heroine. From the beginning Ruth is linked with natural images of freshness and beauty. The flower-ornamented wall-panel in Chapter 1 'initiates a pattern of images and symbolic acts which obliquely reinforce Ruth's supreme innocence' (Crick 1976: 89) – for instance, the 'stately white lilies, sacred to the Virgin' (*R*: 6), the 'snowy-white', 'perfect', 'pure' camellia given to her by Bellingham (pp. 17–18), or the 'white-scented stars' of jessamine, 'her mother's favourite flower' (pp. 139, 49). This sequence is 'perfectly in keeping with the romance convention of pure rather than mixed character' (Crick 1976: 90), and thus disconcerting to readers expecting psychological complexity. Yet even this emphatic imagery sustains contradictory readings.

Elizabeth Gaskell was confident in her defence of the young Ruth because Unitarians denied original sin (see above, Ch. 3 (4)) and found congenial images of uncorrupted childhood in Romantic poetry. The startling fact in *Ruth*, however, is that the sequence of 'innocent' imagery contains sexual elements and is not broken by the sexual act. Ruth's seduction comes after a glorious country walk to her old home, where the cottage flowers are associated with Ruth's mother, but also with the rising sap of spring: 'She wound in and out in natural, graceful, wavy lines between the luxuriant and overgrown shrubs, which were fragrant with a leafy smell of spring growth' (p. 49). Ruth and Bellingham 'sauntered through the fragrant lanes, as if their loitering would prolong the time and check the fiery-footed steeds galloping apace towards the close of the happy day' (p. 44). The 'fiery-footed steeds' from the speech in *Romeo and Juliet* (III, ii, 1), where Juliet looks forward to her wedding night, suggest the inevitability of sexual consummation, but, after her seduction, Ruth still appears' "very modest and innocent-looking in her white gown"' (R: 70). While they are 'living in sin', Bellingham crowns her with water-lilies:

> She stood in her white dress against the trees which grew around; her face was flushed into a brilliancy of colour which resembled that of a rose in June; the great, heavy, white flowers drooped on either side of her beautiful head, and if her brown hair was a little disordered, the very disorder seemed to add a grace. (R: 74)

This daring union of the red rose of erotic love with the white lily of innocence recalls Blake's engravings for

'The Blossom' and 'Infant Joy' in *Songs of Innocence*. The water-lily scene suggests what Blake consciously acknowledged, that if children are innocent of sin, their innocence must include innocent sexuality. The most glaring gap in *Ruth* is the seduction scene itself, but Ruth seems not to have suffered the trauma we might expect (see Easson 1979: 118). Her relaxed behaviour in Wales leads us to assume that the crucially absent London scene is one of happy, though illicit, sex. This inference, however, could not form part of Elizabeth Gaskell's conscious intention. Unitarians were theologically radical, but could not condone fornication. The implications of the water-lily scene must be repressed by Mr Benson's structure of penitence. The red rose vanishes from the flower-sequence, to be replaced by the snowdrops and jessamine of maternal chastity (pp .136, 139, 160). 'After five years', Ruth's 'clear ivory skin . . . was as lovely, if not so striking in effect, as the banished lilies and roses' (p. 207). The concept of 'innocence' as an absence of original sin thus leads to Blakean conclusions which cannot be voiced within Victorian Christianity.

The flower imagery, however, also figures in a more conventional concept of 'innocence'. Victorian moralists routinely used 'spoiled-flower' imagery for fallen women:

'You good gentlemen pick the flowers, and when you have had as much of the sweet as you want, you fling them away in the road.' (Froude 1847: 233)

The rose is torn from its parent stem in all its pride of beauty; the jessamine is scarcely permitted to blossom before it is plucked; and no sooner are their beauties faded, than the merciless hand which was eager to obtain them throws them away with contempt. (*NFI*: 2–3)

Far among the moorlands and the rocks,–far in the darkness of the terrible streets,–these feeble florets are lying, with all their fresh leaves torn, and their stems broken. (Ruskin, 'Of Queens' Gardens', para. 94)

These passages stress the inanimate helplessness of the 'feeble florets', vulnerable to male predation. Peter Cominos demonstrates how this unconscious vulnerability was the prescribed state for middle-class Victorian girls: 'According to the respectable theory, all children were pure and innocent but inherited a fallen nature' which, left to itself, 'speedily developed' (Vicinus 1974: 158). For the Victorians, sexual desire was the most prominent and dangerous symptom of original sin, and children, girls in particular, were protected from this undesirable 'development' by a conspiracy of silence, which kept them ignorant of their own sexual nature. This artificial innocence is incompatible with self-responsibility:

Moral responsibility presupposed freedom of choice as well as the knowledge of moral alternatives. Victorian culture and the genteel family withheld the knowledge from their daughters and their responsibility for choosing . . . As a state of repressed consciousness, innocence absolved daughters from the exercise of responsibility. (p. 161)

The idea that girls must not be allowed to know what it is they must avoid justifies parental authoritarianism: 'While children were still in the nursery, it was advisable for mothers, according to Miss Sewell, to "take the trouble to make and maintain a few regulations which concern their delicacy and purity". . . . What was aimed at was not "comprehension, but obedience"' (p. 158). This notion of innocence as repressed consciousness exactly accounts for Ruth's early response to Mr Bellingham. As

Crick puts it, 'the intermittent, confused, and hopelessly childlike promptings of Ruth's as yet unformed moral sense . . . simply disqualify her as a morally responsible person' (Crick 1976: 93). As a general educational practice, Elizabeth Gaskell was opposed to the kind of authority-and-dependence structure which maintained this girlish innocence. *Ruth* sets up a strong contrast between the authoritarian Bradshaw and the more flexible Benson household, in their education of boys:

> If another's son turned out wild or bad, Mr Bradshaw had little sympathy; it might have been prevented by a stricter rule, or more religious life at home. . . . All children were obedient if their parents were decided and authoritative; and every one would turn out well, if properly managed. (*Ruth:* 209)

Leonard's education, on the other hand, is undertaken as 'a series of experiments' (p. 201) with 'self-dependence' as the aim (p. 120), and the Bensons see as a 'hopeful' sign 'the determination evident in him to be a "law unto himself" ' (p. 380), a phrase which Elizabeth Gaskell uses approvingly of her own daughter (*L* 101).

These two educational approaches produce different attitudes to wrong-doing. When Richard Bradshaw commits a crime, the authoritarian father attributes it to '"innate wickedness"' (*R:* 401) and sees his parental duty as punishment (pp. 397, 400). Mr Benson, on the other hand, in a response which Noddings (1984: 36) and Gilligan (1977: 513) define as 'feminine', wants to know '"all the circumstances"' (*R:* 401) before he decides what to do. Carol Gilligan quotes a modern American woman as epitomising this attitude: 'everybody's existence is so different that I kind of say to myself, that might be something that I wouldn't do, but I can't say that it is right or wrong for that person. I can only deal with what is appropriate for me to do when I am faced with specific problems' (quoted in Gilligan 1977: 513). Elizabeth Gaskell's own position is extraordinarily similar: 'I am more and more convinced that where every possible individual circumstance varies so completely all one can do is to *judge* for oneself and take especial care *not* to judge other[s] or for others' (*L* 424). In this context her remark to George Eliot – 'I wish you *were* Mrs Lewes. However that can't be helped, as far as I can see, and one must not judge others' (*L* 449; cf. 451) – appears not as 'holier than thou' but as genuinely non-judgemental.

Ruth is similarly radical in approving Benson's non-judgemental attitude not only to the erring son but also to the 'fallen woman', and in condemning Bradshaw's 'principled' rejection (*R:* 347). But the novel is inconsistent in its attitude to the causes of Ruth's fall. Since harsh judgement is seen to derive from an authority/obedience model of parent–child relations, the approved non-judgemental attitude should be linked with the opposite belief in education for moral independence. Yet Ruth's 'fall' is attributed not to the protected upbringing which 'disqualif[ies] her as a morally responsible person' (Crick 1976: 93) but, paradoxically, to a failure of parental vigilance. In Chapter 3 Bellingham tells Ruth to 'judge for [her]self' (p. 43) whether to spend the day with him. The confused paragraph which follows veers between apologising for Ruth because 'she was too young when her mother died to have received any cautions or words of advice respecting *the* subject of a woman's life', and doubting whether 'wise parents ever directly speak of what, in its depth and power, cannot be put into words – which is a brooding spirit with no definite form or shape that men should know it, but which is there, and present before we have recognised and realised its existence' (*R:* 43). Brian Crick finds 'the

unpleasant tone of puerile religiosity in this quotation . . .
beyond apology' (Crick 1976: 93), but I would argue that
the inflated vocabulary and broken syntax signal the
author's distress at having to evade, in this tabooed area,
her general assumption that children should judge for
themselves. The passage demonstrates how female
sexuality, being ideologically 'unspeakable', cannot be
brought into consciousness for the daughter, who is
therefore unable to take a moral position. In the next
chapter Ruth's seduction is blamed on Mrs Mason's
failure, *in loco parentis*, to exercise 'tender vigilance and
maternal care' (p. 53).

Whether Ruth's innocence is a Blakean absolute or a
state of repressed consciousness, it is clear that her 'fall'
occurs not with the sexual act but with its articulation, in
moral terms by the little boy who calls her '"a bad,
naughty girl"' (p. 71), and in social terms by Bellingham's
desertion, which makes her a 'hunted creature' (p. 95)
and 'an outcast' (p. 99). From this point Ruth's
consciousness is split between an ideological surface
articulated in moral and social terms, and an inarticulate
sub-text of metaphors and dreams. Her desire for
Bellingham does not cease but becomes 'a nightmare' (p.
92). Her mind is possessed with a 'storm-spirit' which
'rent and tore her purposes into forms . . . wild and
irregular' (p. 99).

In the course of the novel Ruth comes under the
protection of a number of surrogate parents, who can be
grouped, irrespective of sex, either with the maternal,
caring principle or with the paternal rule of law. Ruth's
guardian, Mrs Mason, and Mrs Bellingham all discharge
their responsibility to Ruth in legalistic terms, by the
payment of money and voicing of moral principles. On
the other hand, Ruth's dead mother acts as a touchstone
of 'proper' maternal care. Mr Benson, who speaks not in

the name of the Father (p. 99) but '"in your mother's name"' (p. 100), is associated with this 'gentle, blessed mother' (pp. 96, 140) and with his own 'gentle mother, from whom [he] derived so much of his character' (p. 134). The maternal bond is flexible, non-judgemental and reciprocal. For instance, when Benson runs to save Ruth from suicide, he falls, whereupon she returns to take care of him. Later he resumes the caring role (pp. 96–100), which enables her in turn, to be a good mother to Leonard and the Bradshaw girls. In these respects it is preferred to the paternal rule epitomised by Bradshaw, which Lansbury calls 'a model for hypocrisy, neurosis and crime' (Lansbury 1975: 65).

Like Ruth's mother, however, Benson assumes that where sexuality is concerned, 'maternal care' must include 'tender vigilance'. In spite of his general commitment to education for self-responsibility, he assumes that his duty to Ruth is to reconstruct a facsimile of girlish innocence. The lie passing her off as a widow effectively denies her positive desire for Bellingham, since a married woman would be assumed to have conceived her child in the state of 'sexual anaesthesia' (Vicinus 1972: 39) which Greg and Acton describe as normal (Greg 1850: 457: Trudgill 1976: 56). The lie creates a new conspiracy of silence, making her experience 'as if it never was'.

Benson's motive in telling the lie is to protect both Ruth and the unborn child, though we are told explicitly that this protective impulse conflicts with his intention to teach the child self-sufficiency (*R:* 120–1). For Ruth, whose sexual life has become unspeakable, a 'horrible dream' (p. 93) which deprives her of 'all power of . . . utterance' (p. 101), respectable motherhood offers escape into the coherent world of her own childhood.

Dutifully, she reproduces for Leonard the vigilant

protection she has herself experienced: 'she fondly imagined [that] . . . she could guard [him] from every touch of corrupting sin by ever watchful and most tender care. And *her* mother had thought the same . . . and thousands of others think the same' (p. 160). This story proves them wrong; both Leonard and Jemima are more ethically secure when they know about Ruth's past than when in a state of childish deception. But such knowledge seems 'unspeakable'. Ruth represses her Blakean memories of sex, which emerge as 'a brooding spirit . . . [whose] depth and power cannot be put into words' (p. 43), a nameless threat to her child. On the night of Leonard's birth she dreams he is 'dragged . . . into some pit of horrors' (p. 162). At his christening, she 'pressed him to her, as if there was no safe harbour for him but in his mother's breast' (pp. 179–80). When they are parted, they dream of one another. 'Her dream of him was one of undefined terror' (p. 255), whereas he dreamed that 'she kissed him, and then spread out large, soft, white-feathered wings . . . and sailed away through the open window' (p. 256). Crick complains that 'Ruth's tortured inner life makes it impossible for the reader to credit the quasi-symbolic function the authorial voice proclaims for this mother's love' (Crick 1976: 103), but this pair of dreams makes it clear that the protective angel/mother, who takes it upon herself to guard her child from all evils, does so precisely by repressing her own knowledge of sex, creating tortured irruptions of undefined terror.

This adult repression, however, is less complete than childhood 'innocence'. What is mostly 'a bad, unholy dream' sometimes seems 'a strange, yearning kind of love' (p. 190). When Bellingham/Donne reappears at Abermouth, Ruth thinks of him as her '"darling love"' and complains, '"They think I have forgotten all, because

I do not speak"' (p. 270). The storm-sequence in this chapter (Ch. 23) echoes that after Bellingham's desertion (p. 99). She is thrown back into the world of nightmare; 'it seemed as if weights were tied to her feet . . . it was so long, so terrible, that path across the reeling sand' (p. 266). 'It was like a nightmare, where the evil dreaded is never avoided . . . but is by one's side at the very moment of triumph in escape' (p. 277). Normal speech again seems beside the point (p. 267) and her social calm is a mere surface: 'quietness it was not – it was rigidity' (p. 269). Her inner turmoil is rendered in images more familiar in *Jane Eyre:* 'her heart felt at times like ice, at time like burning fire' (p. 269) and thumped like 'the sound of galloping armies' (p. 270).

Since these storm and nightmare images first appear after Bellingham's desertion, when her sexuality is publicly defined as 'evil', we can assume that their reappearance at Abermouth marks a renewed struggle with sexual desire. But this time, as the 'stern guardian of her child' (p. 270), she is able to see that Bellingham's sexual self-indulgence, which created her desire, also disqualifies him as a husband and father. Her genuinely tragic situation is expressed as a divided consciousness which threatens madness:

> 'Oh, my God! I do believe Leonard's father is a bad man, and yet, oh! pitiful God, I love him; I cannot forget – I cannot!'
> She threw her body half out of the window into the cold night air. The wind was rising, and came in great gusts. The rain beat down on her. . . . The wild tattered clouds, hurrying past the moon, gave her a foolish kind of pleasure that almost made her smile a vacant smile. (p. 271)

Ruth is radical in Victorian terms in challenging the double standard which put all the blame for sexual transgressions on to the woman. Ruth complains that 'the time that has pressed down my life like brands of hot iron, and scarred me forever, has been nothing to you' (p. 300). She even suggests that Bellingham is more guilty than she is (pp. 270, 300). But the ideological definition of sex as evil means that she cannot make a qualitative distinction between her sexual 'sin' and Bellingham's ethical wickedness. Bellingham, who was sexually conscious and morally responsible when he seduced and deserted Ruth, is ethically culpable in a way that she is not, yet the ideological language of 'sin' makes it impossible for her to separate herself from him, except through the mechanism of 'repentance' (p. 271), which involves rejecting her own sexuality. Branded as evil and banished from consciousness, its memory, 'haunts and haunts' her (p. 300). Although, like other female speakers in Elizabeth Gaskell's stories, she speaks in 'a high tone of quiet authority' when conscious of her moral rightness (p. 278; see above, Ch. 3 (4)), she gains no sense of ethical dignity from rejecting Bellingham's proposal of marriage. In spite of the courage and independence involved in this decision, she is left desolate and confused, still implicated in their joint 'sin':

> the expanse of grey, wild, bleak moors, stretching wide away below a sunless sky, seemed only an outward sign of the waste world within her heart, for which she could claim no sympathy;-for she could not even define what its woes were; and, if she could, no one would understand how the present time was haunted by the terrible ghost of the former love. (pp. 301-2)

What is ideologically 'nameless', 'undefined', 'unspeakable', can only emerge as ghoul or nightmare. When Jemima learns about Ruth's past, 'the diver, down in an instant in the horrid depths of the sea, close to

some strange, ghastly, lidless-eyed monster, can hardly
more feel his blood curdle at the near terror than did
Jemima now' (*R*: 320). When Mr Bradshaw discovers
Ruth's deception, the same image recurs: 'It was of no
use; no quiet, innocent life – no profound silence, even to
her own heart, as to the Past; the old offence could never
be drowned in the Deep; but thus, when all was calm on
the great, broad, sunny sea, it rose to the surface, and
faced her with its unclosed eyes and its ghastly
countenance' (p. 333). With the lie exposed, and the
lidless monster out in the light of day, we might hope
that Ruth could come to terms with her 'terrible ghost'.
But the last section of the novel, in which 'Ruth . . . is
marched dutifully through a supererogatory cycle of
suffering at the hands of small-minded provincial
bigotry' (Crick 1976: 104), demonstrates that female
sexuality can never be anything but a ghoulish
nightmare in the language of patriarchal religion,
because the only proper response to visible sex was
repentance – that is, repression. This demonstration was
not, of course, Elizabeth Gaskell's intention. When she
set up the Benson/Bradshaw debate on 'the fallen
woman', she conceived it as a debate within Christianity;
humane Uniterianism versus punitive Calvinism. In her
anxiety to present Ruth as a 'good woman', she relies
heavily on the language of the Bible. Yet from the
beginning there are indications that this biblical language is inadequate to Ruth's experience. The old
servant Thomas, wishing to warn Ruth of her sexual
danger, can only say, '"My dear, remember the devil
goeth about as a roaring lion, seeking whom he may
devour; . . . " The words fell on her ear, but gave no
definite idea' (p. 50). When Benson first speaks to her in
God's name, his '"words do not touch her"' (p. 99).

After Leonard's birth, Ruth's identity as 'good woman'

is consciously constructed in biblical terms (see Wheeler 1976: 153, 159). The birth is called an 'advent' and associated with Milton's 'On the Morning of Christ's Nativity', and with Matthew 18.10 (R: 159). Ruth's maternal vigilance is compared with that of Rizpah (II Samuel 21.10; R: 207). The poor man's comment on Ruth as a nurse (R: 425) echoes Psalms 4.6 and Revelation 18.10, 15 and 17, while the words '"many arose and called her blessed"' (R: 426) are from Solomon's definition of the virtuous woman in Proverbs 31.28.

These allusions gather momentum with the progress of Ruth's 'redemption', but there is persistent awkwardness in the use of biblical language to refer specifically to Ruth's sexual fault. The biblical image of the Magdalen, with her never-ending tears of penitence, conflicts with the Unitarian idea of successful self-redemption, and Phineas Fletcher's 'Hymne', 'Drop, drop, slow tears!', which prefaced the first edition of *Ruth*, was later omitted (see Wheeler 1976: 150-1). The parable of the Prodigal Son, on the other hand, which gives a more joyful image of the repentant sinner (Luke 15.13–32; R: 95, 178), evades the question of a specifically sexual 'sin'.

The Bible does not help Ruth to tell Leonard about her past; 'she could not find words fine enough, and pure enough, to convey the truth that he must learn' (p. 339), and Benson finds that the patriarchal language of Christianity will not express the 'maternal' impulse he felt towards Ruth; 'words seemed hard and inflexible, and refused to fit themselves to his ideas' (p. 451). Even the ultimate promise that 'God shall wipe away all tears from their eyes' (*Revelation* 7.17; R 453) depends on a structure of sin and penitence which seems increasingly inappropriate to Ruth's saintly existence.

As a 'cultural script' the Bible casts Ruth as 'repentant

sinner' and allows her to 'speak' not in words but in tears. Susan Gubar writes that 'women have had to experience cultural scripts in their lives by suffering them in their bodies' (in Abel 1982: 81). According to Wheeler (1976: 154–7), the scenes at Abermouth represent Ruth's rejection of sin (the 'house built on sand') and acceptance of the Christian life (the 'house built on rock'). But her response to re-entering the house on the rock is to fling 'her body half out of the window' (*R* 271). Her Christian rejection of Bellingham/Donne leaves her 'blind', 'stunned', 'dizzy', suffering 'intense bodily fatigue' (p. 301). She is 'stiff' like 'a sleepwalker' (p. 302). In 'Language and Gender', Cora Kaplan argues that women's relation to language has two poles; at one extreme there are female subjects construed within the male-centred tradition, and at the other, language itself, open to subversion by female experience. Like much of women's writing, *Ruth* is 'a dialectic between those two poles' (Kaplan 1976: 36) – the biblical construct of the virtuous woman, and the unassimilated experience of the body, expressed in terms of physical dis-ease.

For much of the novel the two aspects of Ruth are kept in painful equilibrium, but the 'fever' that she 'catches' from Bellingham/Donne, and which finally overwhelms her, is not only typhus but, metaphorically, sexual desire. If this sounds fanciful, consider the following quotation from *The New Female Instructor*:

Harmless, unmeaning gallantry, is one of the qualifications of a well-bred man. . . . [The unwary girl] forgets that . . . to hear him, is immodest; to be pleased with him, wicked; and that, if she does not fly in time, she will catch the flame that is kindled in *him*, and perish in it for ever.

You may as well, upon the confidence of a sound

constitution, enter a pest-house and converse with the plague. (pp. 56–7)

In *Ruth* also, sexuality appears as sickness. In the inn before her seduction, 'the room whirled round before Ruth; it was a . . . strange, varying, shifting dream . . . strangest, dizziest, happiest of all, there was the consciousness of his love. . . . Her head ached' (p. 58). In Wales Bellingham is delirious, and at Abermouth Ruth hears his voice, 'which she had last heard in the low muttering of fever' (p. 266). Mr Davis calls him 'this fine sick gentleman' (p. 443) as if the sickness were inherent. At Abermouth the parental imperative enables Ruth to resist contagion, but when Bellingham/Donne appears for the third time, Leonard has reached puberty and is outgrowing his exclusive need for his mother (p. 314). His knowledge of Ruth's past gives him the basis for self-responsibility; Mr Davis has proposed a satisfactory future for him. The illegitimate Davis, presumably brought up like Leonard by his mother, is one of Gaskell's nurturing doctors, who will perpetuate Ruth's maternal attitudes. Leonard's need 'had kept her mind on its perfect balance'; with its withdrawal, 'fever-mists . . . arose to obscure her judgment' (p. 343). The illegitimate Mr Davis does not use biblical or moral language, but, alone among her friends, asks her, '"do you love him?"', allowing Ruth, after twelve years' silence, to speak aloud; '"How can I help caring for him?"' 437). *The New Female Instructor* argues that the virtuous woman would 'run' (*NFI:* 57) from sexual contagion as she would from the plague, but immediately after her declaration to Mr Davis, Ruth goes to nurse Bellingham, once again 'wild' and 'raging' in his 'mad talk' (*R:* 439).

Critics who are irritated by Ruth's death read it as a

final, punitive requirement in a process of 'redemption' already pushed to the point of canonisation by her nursing in the hospital. I would argue, however, that her death is the desperate result of the failure of that 'redemptive' process, based on 'repentance' which is really repression, to confront Ruth's genuine dilemma, which is that she was led, while childishly irresponsible, into a sexual bond which she can now neither forget nor responsibly continue. When she enters the sick-chamber she effectively commits suicide, not only because of the typhus but because she thus allows the sexual bond to come into consciousness, defying the formula that repentance = repression, without either changing her view of Bellingham's worthlessness or having any way of reconciling desire with judgement. The result is ideological incoherence and madness.

Benson sees madness as a possibility for Ruth from the beginning (p. 119), and at Leonard's christening we are told that their 'future was hid with God' (Colossians 3.3; *R:* 179), a phrase which St Paul uses as a threat of judgement to fornicators, but which the more charitable Wordsworth takes as a promise of mercy to mad people (Wordsworth [1798] 1963: xxviii). The sickroom repeats the crisis imagery of earlier scenes. The 'whirling' inn-room (p. 58), the 'reeling' sand (p. 266) become the 'rocking chamber' (p. 441). The 'ghost of her former love' (p. 302) becomes the 'phantom-face on the pillow' (p. 441). But this time the slackening of parental duty throws the whole burden of resistance on to an ideological notion of 'virtue', which, because it is built on a repression of sexuality, leaves Ruth with 'no real grasp' on the primarily sexual events of her own life, and therefore no sense of her own identity. Bellingham's question, ' "Where are the water-lilies?" ' (p. 442) breaks through her psychological resistance to remembering pre-lapsarian sex. Unable either to resist, or deliberately to accept, her desire, she abrogates responsibility by retreating into a pre-moral world of 'sweet, child-like insanity' (p. 444). 'There she lay in the attic-room in which her baby had been born, her watch over him kept, her confession to him made; and now she was stretched on the bed in utter helplessness' (pp. 443-4). Her mental state constitutes an ideological contradiction in terms: 'though lost and gone astray, she was happy and at peace' (p. 444). Kaplan argues that 'if the subject cannot be located in linguistic abstraction, then . . . words cannot be constructed in an individual discourse. The dislocated subject treats them as things, sounds, associations, and does not use them in a logical pattern to situate himself in his intersubjective (social) situation' (Kaplan 1976: 24). Accordingly, Ruth, 'softly gazing at vacancy with her open, unconscious eyes, from which all the depth of their meaning had fled', retreats to the Kristevan semiotic (Kristeva 1977: 35), singing songs which her mother had taught her, going 'from one old childish ditty to another without let or pause, keeping a strange sort of time with her pretty fingers . . . She never looked at any one with the slightest glimpse of memory or intelligence in her face; no, not even Leonard' (R: 444).

Of all the critics who have written of Ruth's 'unnecessary' death, not one has noticed that she dies insane. Yet her madness signals the failure of the novel's conscious ideological project. Elizabeth Gaskell wrote in Christian terms to make her Christian readers more charitable towards the 'fallen woman' by showing Ruth's original innocence and eventual self-redemption. Yet the novel demonstrates that it is the Christian definition of sexuality as sin which constitutes Ruth's fall and prevents her rehabilitation. Unable to see herself as 'virtuous' because aware of her sexuality, unable to accept her sexuality because unwilling to be 'sinful', Ruth 'could not remember who she was' (p. 440). Her death is not the author's final punitive act, but the novel's unintended ideological *impasse*. As a 'dislocated subject', Ruth has no social identity, and no imaginable future. Her 'future is hid with God'.

The emotionalism of her funeral signals a general faltering of ideology, its inability to 'interpret' the 'dumb and unshaped' feelings people have about Ruth (p. 452). Benson's sermon remains unread; Bradshaw's headstone uninscribed. Leonard's non-ideological statement, '"My mother is dead, sir"', produces in Bradshaw a response which is not put into words: 'he could not speak . . . for the sympathy which choked up his voice, and filled his eyes with tears' (p. 454).

Chapter Seven

North and South (1854)

Lying is done with words, and also with silence.
                    (Adrienne Rich, *On Lies, Secrets, and Silence:* 186)

With *Mary Barton, North and South* is now the most widely
read of Elizabeth Gaskell's works, and we owe its
modern rehabilitation to the Marxist critics of the 1950s,
who saw its significance as an 'industrial' or 'social
problem' novel. This critical mediation, however, means
that we now receive the text together with a consciousness of its short-comings in Marxist terms: its parent–
child analogy for class relations obscures the economic
source of class oppression in the appropriation of
surplus value, and its 'resolution' is a marriage which at
best seems a symbolic reconciliation and at worst a
romantic diversion from the industrial theme.

I want to argue, however, that the novel only appears
inadequate because of the assumption underpinning
Marxist theory that work relations alone provide the
fundamental structures of society. Feminist theory

affirms that gender relations are at least of equal, if not primary, importance and that any intelligent analysis of society or literature must orientate itself on not one but two axes of explanation. In Elizabeth Gaskell's novels the gender perspective is strongly present, but has been discounted because it does not take the recognisable feminist form of concern for women's rights but instead rises from what Temma Kaplan calls 'the bedrock of women's consciousness . . . the need to preserve life' (in Keohane, Rosaldo and Gelpi 1982: 56).

The parent-child analogy for class relations, while inaccurate in economic terms, is powerfully suggestive in gender terms as an ambivalent model for relationships between unequal partners, implying the divergent possibilities of (maternal) nurturance and (paternal) authority, and many Victorian thinkers apart from Elizabeth Gaskell attempted to solve class conflict by integrating these parental qualities into a benevolent authority. The resulting term, 'paternalist', which is often used dismissively of Elizabeth Gaskell's 'industrial' novels, only properly applies, however, to *Mary Barton*.

Because *Mary Barton* stresses the 'feminisation' of working-class life (see Ch. 4, above), it tends to collapse together the axes of class and gender, seeing female/nurturing/working-class as a 'package' in opposition to male/authoritarian/middle-class. The inference from this assumption is that class problems can be solved in gender terms by 'maternal' fathers who see that 'the interests of one [are] the interests of all' (*MB*: 460). Although this solution expresses the spirit of female, working-class nurturance, however, it is embodied in men: the reformed capitalist Carson and the incipient capitalist Jem Wilson.

North and South offers a sharper analysis by seeing class and gender as axes which intersect rather than coincide.

Its male protagonists of both classes are shown as conditioned by masculine codes of conduct which privilege aggression and inhibit tenderness, rendering the notion of the 'benevolent father' suspect. Moreover, the novel recognises class struggle as the product of economic conflicts of interest which are not resolvable, though they can be ameliorated, by benevolence. Whereas *Mary Barton* reaches a solution more symbolic than material, which paradoxically excludes the working-class heroine, *North and South* reveals a situation which requires the active and continuing mediation of its heroine to affirm 'the need to preserve life' in a class struggle expressed in terms of masculine aggression.

Margaret Hale's achievement of this role is, however, impeded by the disabling ideology of 'separate spheres', and her relationship with Thornton exposes how each is inhibited from full humanity by codes of conduct which effectively rest on lies. While Thornton enacts the 'masculine lie' that judgement must not be swayed by sentiment, Margaret acts the 'feminine lie' that modesty overrides all other virtues. Their relationship, which conventional criticism reads as a 'romance plot' offering a false 'resolution' to the 'industrial theme', thus proves to be an essential analysis of the ideologies which structure industrial organisation, dictating why, among other things, class struggle is always aggressive. Their mutual partial emancipation from gender ideology is offered not as a resolution of class conflict but as a necessary step in a political reorientation which would give higher priority to human need and ensure, minimally, that class struggle is conducted in terms of political debate rather than physical warfare.

'The oppressed [are] not slow to learn the lesson of the oppressors', writes Elizabeth Gaskell in *An Italian Institution* (K6: 532), and *Mary Barton*, despite its Utopian ending, shows accurately how an aggressively masculine concept of authority engenders an aggressively masculine revolutionary socialism. *The Communist Manifesto*, for instance, published in the same year, is informed by images of warfare. Where *Mary Barton* showed the quasi-mythic 'fall' of the workers into class aggression, however, *North and South* shows them entrenched. The bestial imagery reserved for authority in *Mary Barton* is here attributed to the workers: Thornton's voice is 'like the taste of blood to the infuriated multitude' (*NS:* 229) and the workers' yell 'was as the demoniac desire of some terrible wild beast for the food that is withheld from his ravening' (p. 232). But the violent bestiality is explicitly related to the refusal or inability of both sides to engage in speech, the specifically human mode of communication: 'the rolling angry murmur [of] . . . men, gaunt as wolves, and mad for prey [was a] . . . wild beating and raging against the stony silence that vouchsafed them no word, even of anger or reproach . . . their noise [was] inarticulate as that of a troop of animals' (p. 233). There is a play on the word 'reason', which degenerates from meaning 'a logically argued case' to meaning 'an enforced cause'. Before the strike, Thornton complains that '"because we don't explain our reasons, they won't believe we're acting reasonably"' (p. 163), but in the riot scene he relies on the soldiers to '"bring them to reason . . . the only reason that does with men that make themselves into wild beasts"' (p. 232). Thus we have a self-perpetuating cycle in which Thornton's refusal to speak creates an adversary whose savage inarticulacy justifies his own substitution of force for reason. Both sides speak of class relations in terms of warfare; Mr Thornton is satisfied that '"the battle is pretty fairly waged between us"' (p. 125); Higgins looks '"forward to the chance of dying at [his] post sooner than yield"' (p. 183). Meanwhile, to Bessy, '"It's like th' great battle o' Armageddon, the way they keep on, grinning and fighting at each other"' (p. 202).

Elizabeth Gaskell does not suggest that verbal communication will eliminate class struggle. The reformed Thornton is prepared to try '"experiments"' to '"bring the individuals of the different classes into actual personal contact"' (p. 525), but his '"utmost expectation only goes so far as this"' – not that they will '"do away with strikes"' but '"that they may render strikes not the bitter, venomous sources of hatred they have hitherto been"' (p. 526). Some readers are disappointed with *North and South* because they assume it attempts more than this (e.g. David: 15, 20). Orthodox Marxists are inevitably disappointed in that they take as 'given' the very premise which the novel seeks to question – that class struggle is necessarily aggressive. For instance:

> men ought to be forced apart *in spite of* their feelings for one another; ... class interests *have* to wreck personal relations .... By temperament and conscious conviction [Mrs Gaskell] was incapable of exploring the tragic possibilities her experience exposed her to; the great *North and South* is the novel that never got written (Lucas 1966: 201)

The imperatives in this statement derive less from class dialectics than from a masculine relish for antagonism. When 'Mrs Gaskell' speaks out against this aggression, she is perceived merely as 'incapable' of seeing the point, taking refuge in 'an absurd piece of evasiveness' (p. 203) and 'laps[ing] into a discreditable sort of paternalism' (p. 204).

Chapter 15 of *North and South*, 'Masters and Men', examines the 'paternalism' argument at some length, discriminating between different patterns of parenthood which might underlie that term. Margaret argues that 'the masters would like their hands to be merely tall, large children . . . with a blind unreasoning kind of obedience' (*NS:* 166), whereas 'a wise parent humours the desire for independent action, so as to become the friend and adviser when his absolute rule shall cease' (pp. 167-8). This notion of the 'wise parent' as a model of acceptable authority still seems condescending, however, unless we realise that none of the authority bodies dealt with in the novel measures up to this standard. The Church, the universities, the law, the army, the navy and the employers are all exposed as complacent, self-seeking and inhumane. This exposure of the fallible nature of authority is the theme which links a number of plot details which are generally read as 'irrelevant' – Mr Hale's honourable defection from the Church (*NS:* 67; cf. W. Gaskell: 22-3), Margaret's refusal to marry an ambitious lawyer, Edith's lazy life as an army wife, Mr Bell's comfortable prevarication with truth (*NS:* 483).

The most forceful and extensive of these parallel situations concerns Frederick Hale, whose justified naval mutiny provides an analogy, more acceptable to middle-class readers with its Robin Hood air of chivalry, for the mutiny of mill-workers. Just as the workers defy their masters for the sake of others – '"they mun have food for their childer"' (p. 201) – so Frederick defies his captain for the sake of the men under hs command (p. 152). The novel's judgement of Frederick is unambiguous; he is 'an outlaw', but he has offended a 'hard, unjust' law (p. 66). Although the newspaper calls him a '"traitor of the blackest dye"' (p. 153) his mother affirms '"I am prouder of Frederick standing up against injustice than if he had been simply a good officer"', and Margaret agrees; '"loyalty and obedience to wisdom and justice are fine; but it is still finer to defy arbitrary power, unjustly and cruelly used – not on behalf of ourselves, but on behalf of others more helpless"' (p. 154). Nicholas Higgins will use the same argument; '"Dun yo' think it's for mysel' I'm striking work . . .? It's just as much in the cause of others as yon soldier . . ."' (p. 183).

Mr Hale, in the 'paternalism' debate in Chapter 15, draws all these analogies together when he says – surely with Frederick in mind – that in industry masters prefer '"ignorant workers – not hedge-lawyers, as Captain Lennox used to call those men in his company who questioned and would know the reason for every order"' (pp. 165–6). Thus authority is perceived as stifling intelligence in workers, soldiers and subjects to the law.

These three aspects of authority converge in Thornton. As a magistrate (p. 349), he controls the police and the army who protect his own class interest: 'punishment and suffering [were] . . . necessary, in order that the property should be protected, and that the will of the proprietor might cut to his end, clean and sharp as a sword' (p. 245). He calls in soldiers (p. 236) and patronises police officers (p. 349); and his magisterial intervention on Margaret's behalf (p. 352), though welcome, recalls Frederick's words about the court-martial: '"evidence itself can hardly escape being influenced by the prestige of authority"' (p. 326).

Elizabeth Gaskell was anything but naïve about the relation between power and justice. When Margaret urges Frederick to stand trial, he tells her that a court-martial is not '"an assembly where justice is administered"' but '"a court where authority weighs nine-tenths in the balance, and evidence forms only the other tenth"' (p. 326). Those who *are* tried are hanged from the yard-arm (p. 154). Frederick's story, usually dismissed as 'pure plot-spinning' (Wright 1965: 144), provides a powerful argument for working-class solidarity. Frederick is heroic but impotent; a handful of men cannot effectively challenge the armed forces and the law.

This vulnerability of the individual is, of course, the *rationale* for trade unions, since 'unity is strength'. Many Victorians, however, like Dickens, who 'sympathised with the underdog', could not stomach the trans- formation of heroic victims into a powerful organisa- tion. Modern critics usually assume that *North and South* is politically 'soft' in this way, especially as it questions the authority of the Union as well as other authorities. Boucher, the would-be strike-breaker, sees the Union as '"a worser tyrant than e'er th' masters were"' (p. 207), and Margaret agrees (p. 296). Her challenge, however, is not left unanswered. Higgins gives a reasoned defence of the Union as '"a withstanding of injustice, past, present, or to come. It may be like war; along wi' it come crimes; but I think it were a greater crime to let it alone"' (p. 296). Margaret later uses the same defence of Frederick: '"to have stood by, without word or act, ... would have been infinitely worse"' (p. 326). Higgins also defends the closed shop:

'Government takes care o' fools and madmen; and if any man is inclined to do himsel' or his neighbour a hurt, it puts a bit of a check on him, whether he likes it or no. That's all we do i' th' Union. We can't clap folk into prison; but we can make a man's life so heavy to be borne, that he's obliged to come in, and be wise and helpful in spite of himself' (p. 366)

Unlike the other authorities challenged in the novel, the Union is proved a 'wise parent', nurturing even troublesome members like Boucher, who would have '"clemmed to death"' without Union help (p. 367), giving reasons for its actions and coercing its members only when reason fails. The Union attempts a rational approach to class conflict; the strike is planned as legal and non-violent (p. 259), and it is Boucher's dissident faction which provokes the riot. Yet the rioters only act out the aggression inherent in Higgins's own metaphors, which are derived from the dominant ideology; the relationship between classes is ' "like war' " (p. 296) because its terms are dictated by those who maintain their power by force.

It is often said that despite its naïve idealism, *Mary Barton* has a raw, indignant identification with the workers which is lacking in *North and South*, which is read as an *apologia* for owners. I think that this is very far from the truth and that *North and South* focuses on mill-owner rather than worker precisely because Elizabeth Gaskell has recognised the workers' impotence to control the terms of the class struggle; heroic and justified as they are, they have no option but to adopt the aggressive, confrontational position forced on them by the dominant class.

It is for this reason that *North and South* not only examines the motives of the mill-owner who does control the terms of the struggle but also focuses on a woman who is able to challenge him from a position on the intersecting axis of gender. Although Thornton feels no obligation to his workers, he does feel a 'duty ... to explain' to Margaret (p. 125), and her role as 'mediator' consists largely in urging communication between the two sides (*NS*: 232, 383). This emphasis on speech only appears facile and sentimental (David 1981: 43; Lucas 1977: 1) if we read it as a *solution* to class conflict; there is nothing absurd in Margaret's wish that the conflict be enacted in human not bestial ways.

Critics who concentrate on Margaret's role in the novel, however, tend to read it as a *'Bildungsroman'* (Dodsworth, *NS*: 26) rather than an 'industrial novel', and hence to reverse the 'social' and 'romance' priorities. Dodsworth, for instance, sees 'the theme of industrial unrest . . . [as] subordinate to . . . the lovers' relationship' (p. 18) – a reading which limits the interests of a 'heroine' to 'love'. But Margaret's insistence on 'speaking out' gives her a public role and stature. When she prays, 'alone . . . in the presence of God . . . that she might have strength to speak and act the truth for ever more' (p. 503), what we hear 'is not the voice of a Victorian heroine but a Christian hero' (Lansbury 1975: 116). Moreover, while the *Bildungsroman* reading suggests growth from immaturity, the novel presents Margaret from the beginning as a strong woman.

She is explicitly contrasted with Edith, who has fallen asleep on the first page, and like Titania, the Sleeping Beauty and Cinderella (*NS:* 35, 40, 41), waits to be rescued from maidenly inertia by a handsome prince. These early chapters serve to dissociate Margaret from the feminine preoccupations of dress and weddings. Instead of sleeping on sofas, Margaret stands 'upright and firm on her feet' (p. 83); she 'tramp[s] along' (p. 48),' 'out of doors' (p. 50) 'with a boundless fearless step' (p. 110). She makes decisions not only for herself but also for others; she arranges the move to Milton (p. 89) and supplies the 'quiet authority' (p. 85) her parents lack. Her father is 'feminine' (p. 121) and 'delicate' (p. 313), and throughout her mother's illness she has 'to act the part of a Roman daughter, and give [him] strength' (p. 308). While father and brother 'were giving way to grief, she must be working, planning, considering' (p. 318). Though her father's fallibility leaves her 'stunned and dizzy' (p. 74), she learns to 'bear the burden alone. Alone she would go before God. . . . Alone she would endure' (p. 359). Although everyone relies on her, Margaret is 'not a static guide for men's behaviour, not an angel in the house' (Lansbury: 115). She is called an 'angel', but 'a strong angel' (NS: 188, 201, 316), and her role is so strenuous that after her mother's death she finds it 'almost stunning, to feel herself so much at liberty' (p. 425).

It is this strength of character–honest, brave, responsible, straight-looking and straight-speaking– which equips Margaret to urge straight speaking on Thornton and Higgins. Her opportunity comes in the riot scene where she urges Thornton to speak to the men. What happens now is that the smooth flow of the narrative seems to hit a snag, an eddy; what Virginia Woolf calls the 'foam and confusion' which results when a woman novelist dashes against 'something . . . which it was unfitting for her as a woman to say' (in Barrett 1979: 61). Seeing that he is likely to be hurt, Margaret flings herself in front of Thornton with her arms around his neck.

Margaret's motive in defending Thornton is humanitarian, and she is outraged by those who can interpret a woman's action only in sexual terms and assume– '"what proof more would you have?"' (p. 246)–that she is in love with him. In her anxiety to refute this imputation, however, she grossly overstates her indifference, and, as Thornton perceives, she maintains 'maidenly dignity' at the price of being '"unfair and unjust"' (p. 254). P.N. Furbank, in 'Mendacity in Mrs Gaskell', complains that the author seems to be 'in collusion with her heroine. . . . This might be some spy-story, so much do we feel that all depends on Margaret's quick thinking and deceiving the enemy' (Furbank 1973: 54). The snag in the narrative arises because a heroine who has been praised above all for speaking '"plain out what's in her mind"' (NS: 367) now finds herself bound by the duplicitous ethic of the

'virtuous woman' who must avoid sexual shame, while
not appearing to be aware of what it is she must avoid.
As in *Ruth*, the conflict between a general ethic of truth-
telling and the deception involved in maidenly modesty,
produces extreme imagery. Margaret is so sensitive to
the 'ugly dream of insolent words spoken about herself'
(p. 241), the 'cold slime of woman's impertinence' (p.
257), that she is unable to appraise the situation ration-
ally. Her contradictory speech -'"I did some good...
[by] disgracing myself"' (p. 247) - reveals the paradox,
that the humanly ethical action is sexually disgraceful.

She receives Thornton's proposal of marriage 'like
some prisoner, falsely accused of a crime that she
loathed and despised' (p. 252). Even when Henry Lennox
proposed, she 'felt guilty and ashamed of having grown
so much into a woman as to be thought of in marriage'
(p. 65), but the element of publicity in her relationship
with Thornton deepens the shame to the level of
nightmare, again recalling *Ruth:* 'The deep impression
made by the interview, was like that of horror in a
dream; that will not leave the room although we waken
up.... It is there - there, cowering and gibbering, with
fixed ghastly eyes, in some corner of the chamber' (p.
257). The gothic horror of this imagery recalls Freud's
definition of the uncanny as the *heimlich/unheimlich*, the
familiar which has been repressed (Jackson 1981: 65-6).
Margaret cannot allow the knowledge of her sexuality to
come into consciousness; her frantic shame is the effort
at repression, her nightmare imagery the threatened
return of the repressed.

Her denial of a personal motive in defending
Thornton is an unacknowledged lie. Her real lie at the
railway station, however, becomes the focus for
accumulated shame and attracts disproportionate guilt:
'nothing but chaos and night surrounded the one lurid

fact that, in Mr Thornton's eyes, she was degraded' (p. 355). 'Even when she fell asleep her thoughts were compelled to travel the same circle, only with exaggerated and monstrous circumstances of pain' (p. 355). An explicit denial of sexual shame – 'she never dreamed that he . . . could find cause for suspicion in . . . her accompanying her brother' (p. 355) – is followed by words suggesting just that: 'her fall' (p. 356); 'degraded and abased' (p. 358); 'sunk so low'; ' "tempted, . . . fell into the snare" ' (p. 486). It is 'shame' which 'produced a relapse into . . . depressed, preoccupied exhaustion. She gave way to listless languor' (p. 361).

'Shame', then, has reduced Margaret from a fearless girl with 'boundless step' and 'straightforward look' to something like a conventional Victorian lady; 'pallid', 'continually on the point of weeping', she is made to 'lie down on the sofa' (358). More partiuclarly it reduces her to silence. With her father's support she urges Higgins to speak to Thornton (p. 383), but his name causes 'a strange choking . . . which made her unable to answer. "Oh!" thought she, "I wish were a man, that I could go and force him to express his disapprobation . . . " ' (p. 385). When Thornton 'stab[s] her with her shame' by questioning her truthfulness, she 'neither looked nor spoke' (pp. 415–6). After her father's death, 'she lay on the sofa, . . . never speaking' (p. 436), like a 'stone statue' (pp. 437, 461, 463).

Instead of speaking, she begins to blush (pp. 253, 324, 326, 400, 411, 453, 460, 522) – a symptom which Hélène Deutsch links with fatigue and depression as anxiety responses to repressed sexual consciousness (Showalter 1977: 268). Blushing was an acceptable sign of modesty in a Victorian woman – 'a weakness' in man, but 'in woman particularly engaging' (*NFI*: 17) – but it is based on concealment of motives. Ideally, the deception is unconscious (Vicinus 1972: 158), but Fredrika Bremer exposes how daughters 'learned . . . that marriage was the goal of their being; and in consequence (though this was never definitely inculcated in words, but by a secret, indescribable influence), to esteem the favour of men as the highest happiness, denying all the time that they thought so' (Bremer 1843: I, 151–2). Margaret's denial of any personal motive in protecting Thornton, and her denial of being in a sexually compromising situation with Frederick, derive from prescribed standards of 'maidenless'. By 'gazing straight into the inspector's face' and telling her lie – ' "I was not there" ' (p. 343) – Margaret enacts the 'honesty' required of women. 'Women's honor [is] . . . chastity. . . . Honesty in women has not been considered important . . . we have been rewarded for lying' (Rich 1980: 186).

The novel suggests that the values of a 'Victorian heroine' are directly at odds with those of a 'Christian hero' (Lansbury 1975: 116), and that Margaret suffers, psychologically, from having to conform to the former rather than the latter. Yet conventional critics have seen gender as unproblematically polarised in *North and South*. Ganz, for instance, sees Thornton and Margaret as representing 'the particular merits of the masculine principles of severity, self-reliance and authority, and of the feminine instincts of tenderness, dependence, and conciliation' (Ganz 1969: 81). We have seen how 'instinctive' these 'feminine' qualities are to Margaret Hale: they are not innate, but socially constructed, as is Thornton's masculinity. The symmetry which Ganz assumes, is also false, since 'historically, only the masculine experience of separation and autonomy has been awarded the stamp of maturity' (Abel, in Abel *et al.* 1983: 10). The role of language in maintaining this differential is crucial. Masculine power may appear to rest on 'objective' facts such as the control of capital, but this control is itself vulnerable to intangibles such as a 'crisis of confidence' or 'loss of credit'. Masculine, capitalist authority is maintained in the details of interpersonal discourse by distinct linguistic strategies, such as 'abstaining from self-revelation and withholding personal information' (Spender 1980: 47). This denial of human weakness constitutes a 'masculine lie' equivalent to the ideological 'feminine lie', again denying part of the speaker's humanity. Mr Thornton is described as a '"hard man"–not so much unjust as unfeeling' NS: 220)), but we know that this is not the whole of his potential. He can be childlike in enjoyment (p. 121) and maternal in longing to give comfort (p. 339), and when he first visits the Hales, he overrides his usual reserve to explain his career in the human terms which Margaret understands (pp. 125–6).

Subsequent meetings reveal, however, that although he is prepared to speak to her 'in a subdued voice, as if to her alone' (p. 164), about religion and personal relationships, he will not respond to her attempt to speak 'in her usual tone' of both the Bible and of '"strikes, and rate of wages, and capital, and labour"' (pp. 164–5). On public matters he maintains a public manner, explaining industry to Mr Hale 'on sound economical principles . . . entirely logical. . . . Margaret's whole soul rose up against him while he reasoned in this way – as if commerce were everything and humanity nothing' (p. 204). In his Blackwood's articles, Elizabeth Gaskell's father exposes the apparent mathematical certainty of 'political economy' as a cheat. Attacking 'political economists' in their own terms, he shows them to be 'blind guides in the mazes of this science' (Stevenson, August 1824: 210). But although Margaret 'silently took a very decided part in the question' (NS: 216), her indignation remains speechless because it can only be expressed in the 'irrelevant' language of ethics.

Dale Spender argues that 'within patriarchal order we have been locked into thought patterns which are based on the premise[ ] that there is only one reality, . . . based on simple cause-effect relationships' (Spender 1980: 96–7). The advantage of this world-view is that it is 'eminently *controllable*' (p. 97), but it means that 'males have been forced to forgo much of their *human* experience precisely because it is difficult to impose order on' it (Spender 1980: 100). Hence 'human ends have not figured prominently in male meanings because they tend to be disordered, chaotic, inexplicable and beyond control. It is human ends which have traditionally been assigned to women' (p. 100). When Margaret presumes upon Thornton's humanity to tell Higgins to ask him for a job, Thornton tells him to '"tell her to mind her own business"' (*NS:* 398). Both men, but especially Thornton, find it difficult to acknowledge sympathy. 'He had tenderness in his heart . . . but he had some pride in concealing it . . . he dreaded exposure of his tenderness' (p. 403). Higgins, too, conceals his concern for Boucher's '"childer"' behind a masculine bluntness which makes Thornton class him as a 'mere demagogue, lover of power, at whatever cost to others' (p. 396). Although Margaret compares Higgins with 'the wild bird, that can feed her young with her very heart's blood' (p. 204), Thornton cannot believe in this 'tender' motive (p. 398) until he has collected 'evidence as to the truth of Higgins's story' (p. 403). Even then Higgins parades their mutual antagonism as a sort of talisman against womanish sentiment before naming his 'weak spot': '"Yo've called me impudent, and a liar, and a mischief-maker. . . . An' I ha' called you a tyrant, and an oud bull-dog, and a hard, cruel master. . . . But for th' childer,

Measter, do yo' think we can e'er get on together?"' (p. 405). Their relationship remains prickly on the surface but an important trust has been established. 'Once brought face to face ... they had each begun to recognise that "we have all of us one human heart"' (p. 511; see above, Ch. 3 (1)). Thornton, who controls the material practice of production, is convinced that 'actual personal contact' is a necessary check on 'mere institutions' (p. 525)–in other words, that the market mechanism is inadequate to human needs.

Spender argues that the exclusive assignment of 'the human heart' to women:

> is not just unfortunate, it is tragic, for the dominant group which holds the power is disconnected from fundamental human experience. Yet it is the group which legislates on human experience, which defines reality. ... We should not be surprised that we are unable to organize technology towards human ends when human ends have never been part of the pattern of male experience and aspiration. (Spender 1980: 100)

North and South suggests that they should be a part of that pattern. The understanding between Thornton and Higgins is not socialism, but neither is it a sentimental 'reconciliation' in the sense of a cessation of hostilities. It is more like a Geneva Convention aimed at minimising civilian casualties. The Geneva Convention, and the welfare state, are not insignificant achievements in terms of human well-being; yet Elizabeth Gaskell's cautious moves in this direction have been dismissed with surprising vehemence: 'ridiculous and unworkable. ... Gaskell's remedy for discontent ... is a good long talk, preferable round a tea-table' (David 1981: 15); 'human heartedness indeed! If only the matter were *that* simple' (Lucas 1966: 174). Spender, quoting Jean Baker Miller, suggests a reason for all this scorn:

> 'When women have raised questions that reflect their concerns, the issues have been pushed aside and labelled trivial matters. In fact, now as in the past, they are anything but trivial; rather they are the highly charged, unsolved problems of the dominant culture as a whole and they are loaded with dreaded associations. The charge of triviality is more likely massively defensive, for the questions threaten the return of what has been warded off, denied and sealed away – under the label "female"' (Miller, quoted in Spender 1980: 100–1).

'In this context', Spender argues, 'the need for women's silence in patriarchal order should not be under-estimated' (Spender 1980: 101). Even silently, women have some impact on history. Mary O'Brien speculates that 'the historical tendency of women to insist on the survival . . . of . . . their children' may account for 'Marx's most spectacularly erroneous prophecy – the progressive immiseration of the working class. . . . It has been the subsistence relations of the private realm which have provoked the development of the welfare state' (O'Brien: 166). What remains is for this insistence to become vocal: 'for women to affirm the protection of fragile and vulnerable human existence as the basis of a mode of political discourse, . . . to stand firm against cries of "emotional" or "sentimental", . . . would signal a force of great reconstructive potential' (Elshtain, in Keohane, Rosaldo and Galpi, 1982: 145).

Margaret attempts this affirmation, but her single public act ends in humiliation and prevents further communication with Thornton. After his proposal she retreats into maidenly pride and he into manly self-control. He assures her she need not '"be afraid of too much expression [of love] on my part"' 254), and although he dreams of her (p. 410), he is 'too proud to acknowledge his weakness' (p. 411). Her actions at the riot and the railway-station confuse him, so that although publicly he defends her ('"Miss Hale is guardian to herself"' p. 389) – unconsciously he is unable to accept her 'double'nature – 'maidenly' but also articullate and apparently sexually conscious. In *The Poor Clare* Lucy and her demon likeness appear literally as '"that double girl"' (K5: 373; see above, Ch. 3 (Coda)) – just so Thornton has nightmares in which 'he felt hardly able to separate the Una from the Duessa' (p. 411). In Spenser's *Faerie Queene*, Duessa, the Double, the daughter of Falsehood, is a vile creature, deformed below the waist, who traps men by assuming the form of Una, the One Truth, the Christian heroine. Her deformity represents not only women's 'hidden' sexuality but also all those 'disordered, chaotic' elements 'traditionally . . . assigned to women' because they threaten masculine order. 'Tenderness' is as much an enemy of order as sexuality if it is allowed to motivate significant action. Margaret's intervention in the riot is as unacceptable as a caring act as it is as an act of sexual provocation; both are inappropriate to a scene defined in terms of warfare. Immodesty is, however, the easier label to apply, and Thornton bolsters his 'resolute calmness' when Margaret leaves Milton by summoning a conventional 'spoiled flower' image (p. 455).

Back in London, Margaret 'took her life into her own hands...and tried to settle that most difficult problem for women, how much was to be utterly merged in obedience to authority, and how much might be set apart for freedom in working' (p. 508). She claims so much freedom that Edith fears she will become 'strong-minded' (pp. 508–9); the 'work' in question is presumably 'philanthropic activity', which in novels of this date 'provides a gateway to fulfilment outside the home' and 'foreshadows the female emancipation of the decades to come' (Bergmann 1979: 85). Like many Victorian women, she finds that implementing traditional female concerns, preserving life and promoting well-being, leads her to demand feminist rights and powers. In order to transform 'tenderness' into 'work' (which is what philanthropy means), Margaret needs to take hold of masculine power. At the end of the novel she controls Mr Bell's capital and the language of finance.

As for Thornton, whereas at the beginning his '"one great desire"' is '"to hold...a high...place among the merchants of his country"' (p. 160), at the end, his '"only wish is to have the opportunity of cultivating some intercourse with the hands beyond the mere 'cash nexus'"' (p. 525). He wishes to transform work, if not into tenderness, at least into a human activity. Kaplan points out that 'the insights of female consciousness, which place life above all other political goals, have never found expression in a major state or even a political party' (in Keohane, Rosaldo and Gelpi 1982: 75), but Mr Thornton's name and status give him access to national power, through the MP Mr Colthurst, for instance. In this way *North and South* anticipates that strand of modern feminist theory which 'stresses the need to transform society so that men as well as women attribute high value to nurturance (p. 75).

The ending of *North and South* differs from the paternalism of *Mary Barton* mainly in its stress on Margaret's ongoing involvement in the process of social change. In the course of their separate but converging transformations, Thornton and Margaret have challenged the ideological lies which polarise gender identity. Margaret is 'unmaidenly' in initiating their final meeting; Thornton replies in an 'unmanly' voice 'trembling with tender passion' (p. 529). Recollecting the riot-scene embrace, they each retract their previous ideological positions; his 'honourable' proposal now seems 'insolence' (p. 530), while her 'offended dignity' seems 'wrong' (p. 530). The last words of the novel replace the 'loaded' words 'gentleman' and 'lady' (see pp. 217, 253, 520) with 'That man!' and 'That woman!' (p. 530).

This balanced emancipation seems to be the novel's conscious goal; but the most stubborn problem is still with us. When Margaret lifts her head from Thornton's embrace, her face is 'glowing with beautiful shame' (p. 530).

Chapter Eight

Sylvia's Lovers (1863)

" 'Where might is right, and violence is law" '
(Crabbe, *Tales of the Hall*, Book V, 'Ruth')

Sylvia's Lovers is Elizabeth Gaskell's least-known novel,
and its obscurity is usually accounted for by its having
moved away from the 'social-problem' material on which
her reputation mainly depends. McVeagh, for instance,
sees *Sylvia's Lovers* as 'a pastoral love-story set in Whitby
at the close of the eighteenth century, non-political,
non-industrial', 'non-controversial, non-engaged with
social criticism' (McVeagh 1970a: 45, 34; cf. Allott 1960:
19).

Like *Mary Barton* and *Ruth*, however, *Sylvia's Lovers* has
its source in Crabbe's tales of tragedy among the poor.
Crabbe's 'Ruth', in which a girl's life is spoiled when the
press-gang takes the father of her unborn child,
provides both the illegitimate birth in *Ruth* and the press-
gang in *Sylvia's Lovers,* and the line quoted above might
serve as motto for either *Sylvia's Lovers* or the industrial

novels. Lansbury, in fact, sees *Sylvia's Lovers* as 'a necessary preface to *Mary Barton* and *North and South*', since the 'penal laws' of the Napoleonic period, which 'made revolt seem an Englishman's natural right and duty' (Lansbury 1975: 160), set the tone for industrial conflict forty years on.

Because the striking public events in *Sylvia's Lovers* seem incongruous in a 'pastoral love-story', they have been criticised, like many of the short stories of this period, as melodramatic. For McVeagh, the novel's 'sudden lapse into melodrama' spoils its 'leisurely exposition of simple passionate lives in one spot at one point in time' (McVeagh 1970b: 272). This criticism, however, is another example of a mistaken definition producing its own condemnation. *Sylvia's Lovers* is not framed as a purely private story but deals explicitly with the interaction of public and private events. In particular, like *North and South*, it investigates the relation between aggression on a public scale and ideologies of masculinity as manifested in courtship and the family. Like Virginia Woolf, Elizabeth Gaskell perceives 'that the public and the private worlds are inseparably connected; that the tyrannies and servilities of the one are the tyrannies and servilities of the other, (Woolf [1938] 1977: 162).

Where *Sylvia's Lovers* differs from the earlier novels is in giving a historical dimension to these questions; it is charged with a sense of the historical relativity of values, manners, even psychological processes (*SL*: 68, 98, 240, 283, 502), and this too applies at both public and private levels. Just as the Napoleonic Wars lie behind, and structure, the industrial world of the 1840s, so an earlier version of masculinity underlies Victorian gender relations. *Sylvia's Lovers* deals with 'a primitive set of country-folk, who recognize the wild passion in love, as it exists untamed by the trammels of reason and self-restraint' (*SL*: 386), and this passage reveals an important change of emphasis in Elizabeth Gaskell's thinking. *Mary Barton* and *North and South* assume the basic goodness of human nature, which allowed her to see aggression as a perversion, a 'fall', and to distinguish the 'human' qualities of nurturance and reason from 'bestial' violence. In *Sylvia's Lovers*, however, aggression is seen as characteristic of a 'primitive' stage of humanity, where the 'passion' of love easily passes into the 'passion' for revenge. The two influences which converged to produce this change of thought between *North and South* (1854) and *Sylvia's Lovers* (1863) were Elizabeth Gaskell's research for *The Life of Charlotte Brontë* (1857) and the growing impact of evolutionary theory.

The motto for *Sylvia's Lovers* is not in fact taken from Crabbe, but from the 'evolutionary' Section LVI of Tennyson's *In Memoriam:*

> Oh for thy voice to soothe and bless!
> What hope of answer, or redress?
> Behind the veil! behind the veil! [*sic*]

As a Unitarian, Elizabeth Gaskell knew both Lyell, whose *Principles of Geology* underlie this section (*L* 444; Lansbury 1975: 14), and Darwin, whose *Origin of Species* appeared in 1859 (*L* 308; 476). Although Unitarians welcomed scientific innovation, the implications of natural selection were troubling. The idea that people, like animals, were subject to an aggressive 'law of the jungle' challenged everyone

> Who trusted God was love indeed
> And love Creation's final law –
> Tho' Nature, red in tooth and claw
> With ravine, shriek'd against his creed –
> (*In Memoriam* LVI)

Emily Brontë's essay 'The Butterfly', which Elizabeth Gaskell is likely to have read with Charlotte's French *dévoirs* (*LCB*: 234–9), shows a similar anguished doubt about human nature and destiny. 'Why was man created?', asks Emily Brontë. 'He torments, he kills, he devours; he suffers, dies, is devoured – that's his whole story' (quoted in McKibben 1960: 167). The essay could be summed up by the line from *In Memoriam* which Elizabeth Gaskell omits from the motto to *Sylvia's Lovers*: 'O life as futile, then, as frail!'

Elizabeth Gaskell's study of the Brontës' lives and works must, moreover, have forced her to acknowledge the destructive potential of human passion in the details of human relationships. As Ellen Moers puts it, 'we know . . . that all the Brontë virgins . . . loved with brute passion, committed adultery and incest, bore illegitimate children, moldered in dungeons, murdered, revenged, conquered and died unrepentant in the imaginary kingdoms they called Gondal and Angria' (Moers 1978: 172). In an effort to justify these primitive reactions to her contemporaries, Elizabeth Gaskell began her *Life of Charlotte Brontë* with an elaborate exposition of the geographical, historical, economic and political determinants of her subject. *Sylvia's Lovers*, unlike all the previous novels, begins with a similar exposition of 'Monkshaven' life in 1797 – history, geography, class structure, whaling industry and Napoleonic Wars – the point of which seems to be to explain the characteristic aggression of its people. Like *Wuthering Heights*, set at the same period, *Sylvia's Lovers* hinges round the ethic of revenge, which in Monkshaven was 'considered . . . wild justice' (*SL*: 283). The reference here is to Francis Bacon's essay defining revenge as 'a kinde of Wilde Justice, which the more Mans Nature runs to, the more ought Law to weed it out' (*Essays*, No. 4). Thus, if evolutionary theory forced Elizabeth Gaskell to recognise aggression as a primitive or intrinsic feature of human nature, it only intensified her perennial problem: how to curb aggression by a rule of law which was not itself aggressive.

The industrial novels traced working-class violence to frustrated parental love (see above, Chs. 3 (1), 4), and in *Sylvia's Lovers* this process is ritually enacted. In Chapter 2 a crowd, mostly of women, tense with expectant love, awaits the return of sons, brothers, lovers and husbands from the first whaling-ship of the season; 'everybody relied on every one else's sympathy in that hour of great joy' (*SL:* 17). In Chapter 3 the press-gang seize the returning sailors and love turns to bestial rage:

> pressing round this nucleus of cruel wrong, were women crying aloud, throwing up their arms in imprecation, showering down abuse as hearty and rapid as if they had been a Greek chorus. Their wild, famished eyes were strained on faces they might not kiss, their cheeks were flushed to purple with anger or else livid with impotent craving for revenge. Some of them looked scarce human; and yet an hour ago these lips, now tightly drawn back so as to show the teeth with the unconscious action of an enraged wild animal, had been soft and gracious with the smile of hope; eyes that were fiery and bloodshot now, had been loving and bright; hearts, never to recover from the sense of injustice and cruelty, had been trustful and glad only one short hour ago. (*SL:* 29)

Sylvia Robson, an uninvolved bystander, demonstrates the contagion of feeling. ' "When folk are glad I can't help being glad too" ', she says (p. 27), but the 'low, deep growl' of the frustrated women provokes 'her own hysterical burst of tears' (pp. 29–30). At the funeral of the sailor shot by the press-gang she weeps so that

143

people think her his sweetheart (pp. 70-1), and at the sight of wounded Kinraid she feels a vehement 'hatred and desire of revenge on the press-gang' (p. 76).

The law which ought to 'weed out' revenge is instead its provocation. The press-gang invokes ' "the King's name" . . . with rough, triumphant jeers' (p. 215), knowing that their victims will have no opportunity to invoke the laws which should protect them (pp. 6, 216), and in Chapter 23 they trap victims by a shameful trick (p. 256). The press-gang, moreover, epitomises a general oppression. Like Mary Wollstonecraft (W: 161), Elizabeth Gaskell argues that insupportable taxes 'demoralise the popular sense of rectitude' (SL: 99), while 'the law authorities forgot to be impartial . . . and thus destroyed the popular confidence in what should have been considered the supreme tribunal of justice' (p. 168). Far from 'weeding out' revenge, the law seems ' "mad for vengeance" ' (p. 272); Sylvia sees the judge as ' "trying to hang' " her father (p. 333). The 'solemn antique procession' in York Minster which begins the assizes, implicates the Church with the other authorities (p. 309), and Dr Wilson's funeral sermon leaves unresolved 'the discord between the laws of man and the laws of Christ' (p. 67).

'Now all this tyranny . . . is marvellous to us' (pp. 6-7), says Elizabeth Gaskell, with deliberate irony, for the alliance of the law with the armed forces in *Sylvia's Lovers* is the same as in *North and South*. In Milton Northern, magistrates and soldiers combined to protect capitalist against worker. In Monkshaven at the time of the French or 'bourgeois' revolution, the capitalist is at first ambiguously placed between landowner and workers (p. 8), and Philip Hepburn the shop-keeper aligns himself with popular feeling in defying the laws on smuggling. As he emerges as the 'new man' in historical terms, however, he aligns himself more and more with law and order.

In Chapter 4 there is a formal debate about the press-gang between Philip Hepburn, who is one of Sylvia's lovers, and her father Daniel Robson, which defines their different attitudes to legal tyranny – 'legalism' versus 'authentic democracy' (Eagleton 1976a: 22) or Burke versus Tom Paine (Rance 1975: 141). Although John Lucas argues that Robson 'comes out of this exchange much better than Mrs Gaskell intended' (Lucas 1975: 18), the evidence suggests that she knew exactly what she was doing. According to Holt, 'all Unitarians of whom there is any record were in warm sympathy with the French Revolution' and welcomed Paine's *Rights of Man* (Holt 1938: 106, 110). It was a sermon by a Unitarian minister, Richard Price, welcoming the Revolution, which provoked Burke's conservative *Reflections* (Holt 1938: 106–7); at Bolton in 1791 an effigy of a Unitarian minister was burned together with one of Tom Paine (p. 110), and in 1792, the year when Elizabeth Gaskell's father became a Unitarian minister, 'Church and King mobs attacked *Cross Street* Chapel, Manchester, (p. 114), where William Gaskell was later minister. From 1792, Unitarians were 'singled out as special objects of attack' (p. 116) in what Holt calls 'the English Reign of Terror' (p. 115) associated with the sedition trials arising from Tom Paine's writing. All this suggests that Elizabeth Gaskell was likely to support 'democracy' rather than 'legalism'.

Monkshaven democracy, however, is merely an animal-like reflex to institutional force. The 'growl' of the frustrated women goes up 'as a lion's growl goes up, into a shriek of rage' (p. 29); cornered by the gang, Kinraid watches with eyes 'vivid, fierce as those of a wild cat brought to bay' (p. 217) and the mob which burns the

Randyvowse make a noise 'as of some raging ravening beast growling over his prey' (p. 261). Although Daniel Robson, and Charley Kinraid, Sylvia's other lover, seem to represent a primitive kind of populism, while Philip Hepburn represents emergent capitalism, the competition between Sylvia's lovers mirrors a historical conflict in which neither side is wholly admirable, because both rely on force. The 'love story' apparently follows the historical process whereby 'wild passion' gives way to 'reason and self-restraint' (*SL*: 386), but the 'wild cat' Kinraid and the 'prudential, shopkeeping Hepburn' (Rance 1975: 144) share the same basic aggression, structured by different ideologies of masculinity.

Sylvia Robson, whose name suggests 'sylvan', seems a child of nature. She resists formal education, is at home in the cowshed, walks barefoot and is linked with landscape and sea (p. 342), but she is no Catherine Earnshaw. Merry, wilful and talkative, she is nevertheless loving, domesticated and, up to a point, dutiful. Whereas the Brontë heroines evade Oedipal socialisation (Barker *et al.* 1978: 188), the family at Haytersbank conform to the 'normal' Oedipal pattern described by Bardwick (p. 136). The development of Sylvia's character depends on the gender polarisation of her parents.

Daniel Robson's masculinity derives from a decided separation of gender roles. As a harpooner in the dangerous whaling trade, he lived a life never entered by women. Bell Robson, on the other hand, though skilful and energetic, is engaged in the exclusively feminine activities of spinning and dairy-work. As a farmer, Robson maintains this separation, 'a kind of domestic Jupiter' (p. 51), 'to whom . . . none but masculine company would be acceptable' (p. 88).

Although Daniel is childish and impulsive, his wife

allows him to think 'that he ruled with a wise and absolute sway' (p. 247; cf. p. 281), and in Chapter 5, when Daniel derogates woman's company (p. 49) and welcomes even the tailor, because ' "t'ninth part [of a man]'s summut to be thankful for, after nought but women" ' (p. 50), it is Sylvia who has contrived the tailor's visit. Sylvia has learnt the trick of 'managing her father' (p. 49) because she 'hated the discomfort of having her father displeased' (p. 39), but Bell genuinely believes that 'the masculine gender' confers 'superior intellect' (p. 125), and that virtue, in a woman, consists in going 'through life in the shadow of obscurity, – never named except in connexion with good housewifery, husband, or children' (p. 122). With Daniel's death, her own intellect collapses, deprived of its *raison d'être* (p. 321).

Extreme gender polarisation creates an atmosphere in which each sex admires in the other the qualities from which it is excluded, and, like the knights and heroes of old, Daniel uses tales of courageous exploits as ' "t'way of winnin' t'women" ' (p. 105). When Charley Kinraid uses his Greenland tales to recreate in Sylvia the excited, awe-struck atmosphere of her parents' courtship (Ch. 9), the scene recalls Othello's tales of war to Desdemona (*Othello* I. iii).

Philip Hepburn's occupation does not distinguish him from women. He serves alongside Hester in the shop and, in contrast to Kinraid, he is pale and stooping, but although Philip shows the beginning of a change which J.S. Mill notes, 'the association of men with women in daily life [becoming] much closer ... than it ever was before' (*W:* 310), he is not therefore less masculine than Kinraid. Speaking of *Wuthering Heights,* Gilbert and Gubar write, 'many readers have been misled . . . to suppose that the rougher, darker Heathcliff incarnates masculinity in contrast to Linton's effeminacy' (Gilbert and Gubar 1979:280). Linton, however, 'does not need a strong, conventionally masculine body, because his mastery is contained in books, wills, testaments, leases, titles, rent-rolls, documents, languages, all the paraphernalia by which patriarchal culture is transmitted from one generation to the next' (p. 281). Just so, Philip is distinguished from Hester because it is to him, as a man, that the Foster brothers bequeath their capital and the management of the shop, a process ritualised by lengthy stock taking and accounting (Chs. 14, 16). The link between written texts, property and patriarchal ideology is emphasised as Jeremiah Foster 'unconsciously employed for the present enumeration of pounds, shillings, and pence' the 'peculiar tone' normally reserved for reading the Bible (p. 172).

Philip thus represents the law in the Lacanian sense (see above, Ch. 1 (2v)). As an older male relative assumes the right to control Sylvia's indignation against the press-gang: " 'Don't be silly; it's the law, and no one can do aught against it, least of all women and lasses"' (p. 28). He also controls her education. Although he offers to teach Sylvia, he is satisfied when she resists (Chs. 8, 10). Rousseau saw the reluctance of girls to read and write as a sign of their inherent incapacity, but Sylvia rightly sees learning as irrelevant to the sort of role defined by her mother's life.

When, in a now familiar bit of symbolism, Sylvia falls asleep while Philip reads (*SL:* 95), her father invokes a country custom which gives any man a right to kiss a sleeping girl. Sylvia is thus established not as a speaking subject but as a sexual object, appropriately pictured as 'little Red Riding Hood' (p. 87). Similarly, in *Two Gentlemen of Verona* Silvia's identity is constructed in male rivalry:

Sylvia's Lovers (1863)

Who is Silvia? what is she,
That all our swains commend her?
(*Two Gentlemen of Verona* IV. ii)

Sylvia's lovers, however, have very different sexual attitudes. Whereas Kinraid is spontaneous in making physical contact, takes advantage of a kissing game (Ch. 12) and, when Sylvia is upset, 'lulled and soothed her in his arms, as if she had been a weeping child and he her mother' (p. 195), Philip in a similar situation represses the maternal impulse (p. 328), and at the New Year's party his physical confinement, 'wedged against the wall' (p. 148), 'pent up in places' (p. 150), mirrors the sexual repression of the Puritan ethic, in which sexual indulgence is a distraction from righteous labour. Philip allows himself to think of Sylvia only as a reward for industry and thrift.

Although the Gaskells were Nonconformist and subscribed to the 'work ethic', they did not approve of the kind of Puritanism represented by *Paradise Lost* (e.g. VIII, 567–72): 'the translation of God into a divine accountant with his finger on the ledger was a concept alien to all forms of Unitarian thought. . . . To regard sexual desire as inherently evil, the mark of the old Adam, was to defile the whole personality' (Lansbury 1975: 156). Although Philip listens to a 'tempter "close at his ear" ' (*SL*: 329 – a clear reference to Satan 'close at the eare of *Eve*' (*Paradise Lost* IV, 800) – and calls himself ' "one o't'devil's children . . . for the Scriptur' says he's t'father o' lies" ' (*SL*: 479), his temptation is not to indulge but to deny sexuality, and his lie is this denial.

Sylvia's Lovers is the third of Elizabeth Gaskell's novels to hinge around a lie (see *Ruth, North and South*), and each lie derives from a denial of female sexuality. When Philip allows Sylvia to believe that Kinraid is dead he not only

149

makes it more likely that she will marry him but he also
defines her femininity in a way which is acceptable to
him. Sylvia's passion for Kinraid confirms her as a sexual
being, whereas Philip wants her to be a 'pretty, soft little
dove' (p. 335). When he assumes the rights of a brother
to ' "watch o'er ye and see what company yo' kept" '
(p. 210) he is authorised by Sylvia's mother, who sees her
as a child 'to be warned off forbidden things by threats of
danger' (p. 186). Thus, in persisting in his lie, 'he felt like
a mother withholding something injurious from the
foolish wish of her plaining child' (p. 235), perpetuating
the 'protective' parental stance which deprives women
of adult status.

The more Philip is convinced of the strength of
Sylvia's love for Kinraid, the more anxious he becomes

> to convince her that he was dead ... repeating ... the lie that
> long ere this Kinraid was in all probability dead ... that,
> even if not, he was as good as dead to her; so that the word
> 'dead' might be used in all honest certainty, as in one of its
> meanings Kinraid was dead for sure. (p. 329)

For Philip, Kinraid symbolises Sylvia's sexual autonomy,
and he exerts his authority over her to assert that her
independent sexuality is and must be dead if she is to be
his wife. Their marriage is appropriately like a funeral;
Philip 'wedded his long-sought bride in mourning
raiment, and ... the first sounds which greeted them as
they approached their home were those of weeping and
wailing' (p. 340; also pp. 335–6). He regrets what he has
done, and wants 'the old Sylvia back', but 'Alas! that
Sylvia was gone for ever' (p. 330). The text again inverts
an accepted maxim: 'Philip was beginning to feel ... that
the fruit he had so inordinately longed for was but of the
nature of an apple of Sodom' (p. 334). In *Paradise Lost* (X,

560–70), Sodom apples represent indulged sensuality, and William Coulson uses the phrase in this sense (*SL:* 155), but Philip's ashes in the mouth are the result of sexuality denied. ' "Mrs Hepburn" ' leads the life of Curly Locks, a domestic 'idol in a befitting shrine' (p. 341), but at night Philip looks 'to see if she were indeed sleeping by his side, or whether it was not all a dream that he called Sylvia "wife" ' (p. 343).

Sylvia's sexuality, however, is not dead but repressed, and Philip's unconscious desire evokes the figure of Kinraid, who was its visible sign: 'all this time Philip was troubled by a dream ... a conviction of Kinraid's living presence somewhere near him in the darkness' (p. 343). When Sylvia speaks of her own dream of Kinraid, however, he finds it intolerable; ' "what kind of a woman are yo' to go dreaming of another man ... when yo're a wedded wife?" ' (p. 354). Before long Philip is jealous of anyone who receives her love – Hester (p. 349), the baby (p. 356) and even 'the inanimate ocean' (p. 360).

Sylvia, meanwhile, 'was glad occasionally to escape from the comfortable imprisonment of her "parlour" into 'solitude and open air, and the sight and sound of the mother-like sea' (p. 350). Both 'sea' and 'mother' are ambiguous terms in *Sylvia's Lovers*; her mother's sur- veillance, perpetuated by Philip, denies to Sylvia both Kinraid and sexual maturity, but her mother's impulse to succour the needy (p. 484), manifested in Sylvia's effort to save the sinking ship, brings back Kinraid and a crisis of adult autonomy. Like the mother, the sea is the site both of love and death, both of Kinraid's parting pledge and of his disappearance and Philip's denial, and provokes in Sylvia a complication of emotions involving physical and ideological 'death': Kinraid 'was dead; he must be dead; for was she not Philip's wife?' Recalling what Philip said about her dream, she shuddered 'as if cold steel had been plunged into her warm, living body' (p. 360) and when she sees Kinraid again, 'her heart leaped up and fell again dead within her, as if she had been shot' (p. 377). Sylvia's 'death' takes the feminine form of silence. After Philip's 'cold steel' speech 'she lay down, motionless and silent' (pp. 354–5), 'her lips compressed' (p. 355) as Hester's are from long usage (p. 24). 'Nothing stirred her from her fortress of reserve (p. 356), but though 'she said no word', she 'constantly rebelled in thought and deed' (p. 359). Quiet as a Quaker (p. 362), her stillness is the result of 'unnatural restraint' (p. 363). Eventually, feeling that she ' "cannot stay in t'house to be choked up wi' [her] tears" ' (p. 368), she runs out into a storm and, like Ruth, is 'quieted by this tempest of the elements' (p. 369). As in Chapter 3, her emotion is shaped by communal feeling, and as part of a crowd she unwittingly helps save the ship on which Kinraid is returning.

Kinraid's return is the Freudian 'return of the repressed', initially 'unutterable' (heading to Ch. 35) and, as in the conclusion to *Ruth*, madness threatens: she speaks 'with incessant low incontinence of words' (p. 383), and understands only that Philip ' "kept something from me as would ha' made me a different woman" ' (p. 409). Unlike Ruth, however, Sylvia never connived at the lie denying her sexuality. She was 'no prude, and had been brought up in simple, straightforward country ways' (p. 146). The historical setting releases Elizabeth Gaskell from the disabling Victorian concept of innocence which entangles *Ruth* and *North and South*, and allows her to present Philip's Puritan ethic as an imposed ideology. Sylvia's response to Kinraid's return is not shame but indignation, expressed in the crude terms of her father's 'wild justice'. She 'assume[s] to herself the right of speech' (p. 380), and, 'with her cheeks and eyes aflame'

(p. 381), makes a vow of implacable enmity to Philip (p. 383).

Rance notes that 'Gaskell's audience would have been shocked by the sympathy extended to a heroine renouncing her marital vows' (Rance 1975: 139), but several of the short stories following Caroline Norton's *English Laws for Women* (1854) and the Matrimonial Causes Act (1857) show her worried preoccupation with the indissolubility of marriage. In Chapter 3 (4) I argued that Elizabeth Gaskell's approved response to injustice was to 'speak out', but the historical perspective of *Sylvia's Lovers* allows her to see that what seems to be 'the voice of conscience' may be only 'sublimated maxims' (Abel 1982: 49). When Sylvia throws off wifely duty and vows eternal enmity to her husband, she is simply adopting her father's attitude, exchanging one masculine code for another. Sylvia shares the 'settled and unrelenting indignation' (*SL*: 52) which her father felt for the press-gang, and the vow she makes against the witness who hangs her father – ' "I'll niver forgive – niver!" (p. 319) – is the same as she makes to Philip: ' "I'll never forgive yon man, nor live with him as his wife again" (p. 383).

Kinraid's marriage, however, makes her reassess the 'eternal' vows of love and hate which structure the revenge ethic. Her disillusionment with both her lovers makes Hester say that she is ' "speaking like a silly child" but she insists, ' "No. I'm speaking like a woman; like a woman as finds out she's been cheated by men as she trusted, and as has no help for it" ' (pp. 443–4). The law in other words, is not for women.

Philip's pathetic response to Kinraid's return is to 'kill' his 'prudential shopkeeping' self. As Coulson says, "them that's dead is alive, and as for poor Philip, though he was alive, he looked fitter to be dead" ' (p. 399);

Philip's letter instructs them all to ' "look on [him] as one dead" ' (p. 405). Instead, he enlists, reverting to the older pattern of masculinity, the ' "man of peace becoming a man of war" ' (p. 450). The 'flat and alien' battle scenes involving both Philip and Kinraid are not, however, just 'adventitious melodrama' (McVeagh 1970b: 275); lacking the glamour of distance which lies over the Greenland tales, they expose the heroic ideal as childish. Just as Daniel Robson 'had a true John Bullish interest in the war, without very well knowing what the English were fighting for' (*SL*: 95), so the siege of Acre appears 'a series of random heroics' (Rance 1975: 151). Kinraid, taking part in the fighting, knew nothing except 'that the French . . . were trying to take the town from the Turks, and that his admiral said they must not, and so they should not' (*SL*: 427). The death of comrades leaves them 'bright and thoughtless as before' (p. 428), 'as if it were some game at play instead of a deadly combat' (p. 429). Although even Rance assumes that Elizabeth Gaskell approves of this chauvinist war (Rance 1975: 151), it is worth noting that one of her earliest stories appears alongside vehemently anti-military pieces in *Howitt's Journal* (Vol. II), and that Margaret Hale is suspected of sympathising with the Peace Society (*NS*: 299). Surely, too, it is significant that Philip is maimed and disfigured in a purely fortuitous explosion, which, far from confirming his heroic manhood, leaves him sick, poor and unrecognised.

Philip's 'irrelevant sojourn' at St Sepulchre's (Mc-Veagh, 1970a: 275) brings into focus the ideological mechanism which, in the past, has linked aggressive masculinity with subservient femininity. The fable of Sir Guy of Warwick, the soldier-turned-monk who reveres his faithful wife from a distance (*SL*: 465–6), is based on the outmoded chivalry which J.S. Mill describes in *The Subjection of Women* (*W:* 301). Mary O'Brien accounts for such heroic traditions in terms of men's need to synthesise their 'fractured sense of continuity' (O'Brien: 182). Both men and women, as finite individuals, are alienated from larger cycles of birth and death, but for women, this alienation is mediated by the labour of reproduction. Men, on the other hand, transcend their more basic alienation by constructing systems of symbolic continuity – hereditary monarchy, religious ritual, Romantic 'oneness'. 'The contradictions of symbolic continuity are nowhere more visible', she argues, 'than in the chivalric ideal of the Christian knight, who paused to swear fealty to the Virgin Mother before he rode off to slaughter her immaculate Son's sons, in the name of obedience to his bloodthirsty lords, spiritual and temporal' (p. 182). J.S. Mill presents chivalry as 'a remarkable . . . moral ideal' in its time, but argues that 'the changes in the general state of the species rendered inevitable the substitution of a totally different ideal of morality. . . without reliance on the chivalrous feelings of those who are in a position to tyrannise' (*W:* 301–2). Accordingly, the St Sepulchre's chapter is called 'A Fable at Fault', and Sir Guy's story 'a fable of old times', inappropriate to Philip and Sylvia.

Chivalry was always a forlorn hope for Philip; the day after his enlistment 'he found in the dark recess of his mind the dead body of his fancy. . . that he might come home, handsome and glorious, to win the love that had never been his' (*SL:* 392). As a 'self-made man', he is historically a 'hero', not of chivalry, but of the accumulation of capital, which 'does not merely symbolize. . . [but] objectifies continuity' (O'Brien 1981: 182). The crusaders preferred killing to nurturing because feats of arms cemented a self-perpetuating heroic tradition among men. Similarly, because 'capital appears to be objectively self-generating', a capitalist 'hero' will privilege its 'reproduction' over women's reproduction of the species. Philip's Puritan marriage thus 'kills' Sylvia (*SL:* 330), who ' "has no help for it" ' (p. 444). What 'changes in the general state of the species' can resolve this deadlock? George Eliot sees 'the onward tendency of human things' (*The Mill on the Floss* IV.i), as depending on the younger generation, who 'have risen above the mental level of the generation before them'. Elizabeth Gaskell read *The Mill on the Floss* avidly in 1860 (*L:* 462), and the last two chapters of *Sylvia's Lovers* suggest a surge of enthusiasm for this 'evolutionary meliorism' which is then cancelled, as in *The Mill on the Floss* itself, by a contradictory transcendentalism.

The penultimate chapter proposes, in place of revenge heroics and Puritan capitalism, an alternative female ethic based on the value of human life. Little Bella learns her 'first words' not from a patriarchal bearer of the law, nor from an implacably vengeful mother, but from a new Sylvia, who, prompted by widow Dobson, remembers her mother's humanitarian habits. Thus the first words which Philip hears from his child are ' "Poor man, eat this; Bella not hungry" ' (p. 484). Keohane and Gelpi argue that 'the deep-rooted, age-old experience of women in giving and preserving life, nurturing and sustaining', while 'profoundly conservative', is 'also resonant with radical possibilities' (in Keohane, Rosaldo and Gelpi 1982: x). These possibilities are, however, only glimpsed in *Sylvia's Lovers*, which, like *The Mill on the Floss*, loses its dialectical impetus and comes to a trans- cendental standstill.

Sylvia's lovers appear to represent opposed ethics, but the novel shows that each is motivated by self-interest, which is the 'law of the market' as well as the 'law of the jungle'. The women, although they have alternative, generous, ideals, seem to have ' "no help for it" ' but to accommodate themselves to one of these codes. Gillian Beer points out that in evolutionary theory, even the individual who is the vehicle for long-term change is still, as an individual, a 'dead-end' (G. Beer 1983: 43). Perhaps to evade this realisation, the last chapter of *Sylvia's Lovers*, like the end of *The Mill on the Floss*, moves into an alien, mystical mode. The dying Philip rejects the patriarchal heroes – Abraham, David, St John – who have taught him that life is a battle (*SL:* 498) and imagines instead a God like his mother, whose love is soft, like the 'waves lapping against the...shore'. But the forced reiteration of this phrase (pp. 494, 495, 497, 498, 500) suggests some strain. It is no coincidence that it recalls Carpenter's poem 'What Are the Wild Waves Saying?' and the waves as a symbol of eternity in *Dombey and Son* (1848). For the idea of eternity as a transcendent nature/mother, unriven by conflict and unchanged by process, is a peculiarly masculine conception. Women, embodying the physical processes of birth and change, can only speak of feminised nature as transcendent by adopting a masculine voice.

The shattered Philip dies with a glimpse 'behind the veil'; his last word is ' "heaven" ' (*SL:* 500). The novel offers the 'ceaseless, ever-recurrent sound' of 'the waves... lapping up the shelving shore' as evidence of his integration into the symbolic continuities of both Romanticism and Christianity; 'and so it will be until "there shall be no more sea" ' (p. 502). The embedded quotation is from *Revelation* 21.1: 'And I saw a new heaven and a new earth ... and there was no more sea'. Just as Elizabeth Gaskell shows Philip as 'saved' from the errors and difficulties of sex, marriage and fatherhood by fixing his eyes on 'heaven', so Emily Brontë, quoting the same verse of *Revelation* in her 'Butterfly' essay, shows how the destructive caterpillar unexpectedly proves ' "the embryo of a new heaven and a new earth" ' (quoted in Homans 1980: 142). Homans argues that Brontë's 'investment in transcendence' here 'defaces the authenticity' of her work (p. 161): instead of coming to terms with the cycle of death and birth, the essay escapes time by imagining a 'birth' which does not lead to death. According to O'Brien, 'what happens is that the cyclical relation of birth and death [is] replaced by cancelling...death's significance by the magic of *re*birth' (O'Brien 1981: 150).

In *Sylvia's Lovers* there is an 'authentic' recognition of physical cycles when, after her lovers have come and gone, Sylvia sits on the bed supporting both her dying mother and her baby (*SL:* 393). But this perception, that human continuity lies in habits of nurturance passed from mother to daughter, is 'defaced' by 'idealism's metaphysical banishment of reproduction to the heavens' (O'Brien 1981: 170). The real child who feeds her dying father is displaced by a mother-like God.

Chapter Nine

Cousin Phillis (1863)

A tale of lost innocence
(Keating, C: 30)

Written almost simultaneously with *Sylvia's Lovers, Cousin Phillis* seems like a reaction to the intractable problems of evolution, conflict and passion raised in that novel. Evading the problem of aggression, it presents not 'nature red in tooth and claw' but 'man in harmony with nature'. Scarcely more than a short story, it has been called 'almost perfect' (Lerner, *WD:* 16); 'exquisite' (Greenwood, *WD:* 707); 'the most perfect story in the language' (Lucas 1977: 26). For once, Elizabeth Gaskell has avoided the mixed forms of fiction which cause such critical distress, and written in the clearly defined genre of pastoral, with beautiful descriptions of nature and an apparent absence of disturbing problems (McVeagh 1970a: 3). When Wright describes the story as 'simply the round of life at the farm and the stages in the growth and despair of a young girl's love' (Wright 1965: 197), he is concurring with this view, because melancholy is part of the pastoral mode. Empson explains that 'our feeling that Eden must be lost...makes us feel that it is inherently melancholy' (Empson 1935: 187). Because Phillis is 'close...to the natural world' (Allott 1960: 27), and her 'innocence...harmonizes with the unmarred loveliness of pastoral nature' (Ganz 1969: 223), even her suffering has a gentle inevitability (Keating, *C:* 28). Cudden confirms that 'this is what pastoral is about: it displays a nostalgia for the past...a yearning for a lost innocence, for a pre-Fall paradisal life in which man existed in harmony with nature' (Cudden 1979: 490). In the case of *Cousin Phillis*, however, at least some of this enthusiastic melancholy is in the mind of the critical beholder.

Perfection, paradise, is by definition 'timeless', un-changing. But *Cousin Phillis* describes a post-Darwinian world which 'has no place for *stasis*..., pure invariant cycle, or constant equilibrium' (G. Beer 1983: 11). Its references to rural life have the ambiguity of running water, which is always changing while it appears the same. The 'tranquil monotony' of Hope Farm, which made Paul feel as if he 'had lived for ever, and should live for ever' includes the clock 'perpetually clicking out the passage of the moments' (*C:* 242). The seasons which appear to repeat themselves exactly, corn-harvest succeeding hay-harvest, serve to 'date' the 'succession' of human events (p. 267). Hope Farm also includes more obvious change. Mr Holman, the farmer who is also an Independent minister, a classical scholar and a practical mechanic, shows how human culture evolves, retaining the best of the old, like Virgil's weather predictions (p. 233), while accepting scientific innovation (pp. 236–7, 249). Paul, his father the inventor and his friend Holdsworth the railway engineer, are welcomed, implying that traditional agriculture can smoothly accommodate social and industrial change. We only have to think of the rural resistance to the railway in *Middlemarch* to see that, while Elizabeth Gaskell is not presenting a mythic world of pastoral *stasis*, she is giving an optimistic version of evolution, in which natural cycles and the dialectics of history work harmoniously together. The effect is to highlight one unassimilated factor, which is Phillis's growth to maturity.

The attraction of pastoral lies in its apparent closeness to nature, but its characteristic 'yearning for lost innocence' derives, not from nature as defined by Darwin, but from the cultural myth of the garden of Eden. It was Eve who lost human innocence when she became conscious of sexual shame. Critics who accept with pleasant melancholy that Phillis re-enacts this inevitable loss, are confirming not a fact of nature but an ideological concept. Elizabeth Gaskell's brave story challenges this myth by showing that while sexual consciousness is spontaneous, shame is a social imposition.

In 1836 Elizabeth Gaskell wrote a letter describing a visit to her grandparents' farm at Sandlebridge, which is generally taken to be the model for Hope Farm in *Cousin Phillis*. Nature, in this early letter, is joyfully procreative, and she, both as young mother and blossoming writer, is fully a part of its processes:

> Baby is at the very tip-top of bliss.... There are chickens, & little childish pigs, & cows & calves & horses, & *baby horses*, &...sheep & baby-sheep, & flowers–oh! you would laugh to see her going about, with a great big nosegay in each hand, & wanting to be *bathed* in the golden bushes of wall-flowers.... I sat in a shady corner of a field gay with bright spring flowers–daisies, primroses, wild anemones, & the 'lesser celandine', & with lambs all around me... & wrote

my first chapr of W[ordsworth]...and my heart feels so full
of him I only don't know how to express my fullness
without being too diffuse (L 4)

By 1863, however, as mother of four unmarried
daughters, the youngest of whom was Phillis's age, she
was sharply aware of how the Victorian ideology of
innocent girlhood excludes young women from full
maturity. While 'her realistic appreciation of a person's
continuous mental life allows a mother to expect change'
(Ruddick 1980: 353), the Victorian equation of 'innocence' with 'immaturity' imposes an ideological limit to
growth like the thirteenth fairy's gift in *The Sleeping
Beauty*. Though critics take Phillis as a 'child of nature'
(Keating, *C:* 29), her 'innocence' is not that of pre-
lapsarian sensuality, but of careful segregation, inside a
magic hedge, from the processes of time, seasons,
growth and fertility which structure the rural world.

Cousin Phillis begins when Paul and Phillis are both 17,
and by using Paul as narrator Elizabeth Gaskell gains an
unusual perspective on girlhood: equal in age and class,
only gender divides them. In physical and intellectual
terms she is the superior, 'half a head taller than I was,
reading books that I had never heard of' (*C:* 244). In social
terms, however, Paul is his 'own master' (p. 220) in 'the
independence of lodgings' (p. 219), while Phillis has the
status of a child. Paul thinks it 'odd that so old, so full-
grown as she was, she should wear a pinafore over her
gown' (p. 226). Deborah Gorham confirms that 'as a
status category, the girlhood of a middle-class girl could
be perceived as continuing until her marriage....Only
gradually was this definition being replaced by one in
which girlhood was deemed to have been completed
when the individual had matured, physically and
psychologically, into an adult' (Gorham 1982: 13). Phillis

is not perceived as adult, and because marriage is unacknowledged as an end to girlhood, her education is self-enclosed, cut off from future goals. Although she is eager for technical knowledge (*C:* 236, 269), it does not feed into her practical life as for Paul and her father; although her life round the house and farm is active enough, the female models offered by literature do not stress physical or psychological maturity.

Her name derives from a pastoral tradition in which shepherdesses were ornamental objects of idealised love; in *Sylvia's Lovers*, 'the pretty story of the Countess Phillis' is dismissed as a 'fable of old times' (*SL:* 471), irrelevant to modern marriage. Her chosen reading is Dante, whose Beatrice never matures but passes from innocent girlhood to heavenly beatitude. The love of Dante and Beatrice contrasts sharply with that of the peasant lovers in Manzoni's *I Promessi Sposi* – the realistic historical novel which Holdsworth lends her – who survive sexually predatory barons, a depraved nun, famine, war, plague and finally the girl's own superstitious vow of virginity, and are finally married. Holdsworth thinks it '"pretty and innocent"' (*C:* 265), emphasising the gulf between acceptable sexual knowledge for men and girls.

Phillis remains 'a stately, gracious young woman, in the dress and with the simplicity of a child' (p. 228), until the admiring looks of young men force her mother to see her instead as a 'treasure' which needs 'guarding' (p. 246). The pinafores are left off (p. 247), but Paul is amazed when Holdsworth calls her '"a beautiful woman"'; he 'could not banish the pinafore from [his] mind's eye' (p. 261). The artificial perpetuation of her girlhood means that the sexual attraction between Phillis and Holdsworth finds its analogy not in one of the slow processes of nature but in a violent storm (p. 269).

The momentary illumination which allows him to see her as a fertility goddess (p. 272) is, however, dissipated by ideological 'normality'. His sketch of her as Ceres is 'abortive;', producing only a ' "sweet innocent face" ' (p. 276), and he is able to leave for Canada thinking her transfixed in '"pure innocence...almost like the sleeping beauty"' (p. 276). Confident of the magic hedge, he tells Paul, '"I shall come back like a prince from Canada, and waken her to my love"' (p. 276).

The image of the sleeping beauty prevails over that of Ceres because Phillis cannot acknowledge her desire except in brief, involuntary glances (pp. 272-4). The prescribed innocence of girlhood is manisfested in silence and passivity; as the *New Female Instructor* bluntly puts it, 'love should by no means begin on your part; it should proceed from the attachment of the man' (*NFI:* 57). Gorham's conclusion is that 'the ideological constructs of domesticity and femininity decreed that a good girl would never *seek* marriage. During the period between childhood and womanhood, she would simply wait' (Gorham 1982: 53). This ideology means that Holdsworth need not be a villain to make Phillis unhappy. All he need do is to discount the evidence of his own eyes and interpose the accepted idea of Phillis as an 'unawakened' girl. She has no redress, since to complain would be to acknowledge her shameful consciousness. Once Holdsworth has gone, she has no alternative but silence, but her 'straight looks' (*C:* 227-8) are replaced by shame and blushing (pp. 280, 287, 291, 296, 301).

Paul, however, who is presented as socially inept, does not understand that her love is inconsistent with her 'innocence'. Seeing that she is distressed by Holdsworth's departure (p. 283), he seeks to comfort her by repeating Holdsworth's declaration of love (p. 285). She receives it with a mixture of looked rapture and spoken dis-

couragement, and henceforward it becomes 'Phillis's . . .
secret' (pp. 287-8). It is now that she is most vividly
conscious of reciprocated desire that Phillis appears
most idyllically close to nature, 'standing under the
budding branches of the gray trees . . . her sun-bonnet
fallen back on her neck, her hands full of delicate wood-
flowers', imitating the birds' out of the very fulness and
joy of her heart' (p. 289). Paul, prompted to unusual
poeticism, calls her 'a rose that had come to full bloom on
the sunny side of a lonely house' (p. 289) and is reminded
of Wordsworth's 'Lucy' (p. 290). It is this closeness of
Phillis to the natural world which most delights critics,
yet it is bought at the cost of her individuality. Whereas
the young Elizabeth Gaskell maintained a fully human
presence amid the burgeoning of nature, the maidenly
speechless Phillis looks like a rose and 'warbles' like a
bird. Theological, pastoral and Romantic traditions all
encourage this association of women with nature. In
Paradise Lost, newly created Nature is already female (e.g.
VII, 315-6); in Empson's influential book, *Some Versions of
Pastoral*, nature is female, humanity male (e.g. Empson
1935: 187), and Wordsworth's women 'undergo a
dissolution of identity . . . by entering a termless,
semiconscious life-in-death as a part of natural process'
(Homans 1980: 20-1). For the Victorians, images of
'natural' girlhood sustain the idea that girls can be happy
suspended from adult goals and sexual relationships.
Ruskin, for instance, quotes one of the Lucy poems in
advocating a 'natural' education for girls aimed to
produce 'majestic childishness' ('Of Queens' Gardens',
paras. 70-1). Yet Phillis's 'natural' happiness is based on
sexual love and is terminated by the news of Holdsworth's
marriage. The fact that he marries another Lucy (*C*: 295)
suggests that he responded to Phillis as a type rather
than an individual. Although he speaks sentimentally

about the nosegay which he has preserved to 'remind [him] of Hope Farm' (p. 277), he shows no consciousness of the individual pain which the news of his marriage will bring; 'Phillis had faded away to one among several "kind friends" ' (p. 293). Phillis, unable to acknowledge that her happiness had a human cause, can only 'conceal her disappointment' (p. 302) by intensified silence (p. 301), the strain of which produces signs of physical illness (p. 304). Perhaps she reminds Paul of Lucy because 'the Lucy poems image a feminine figure for whom there is no discontinuity between imaginative sympathy with nature and death, and a masculine speaker for whom Lucy's death is non-catastrophic, sanctifying nature as well as darkening it' (Homans 1980: 21).

As in *Ruth, North and South* and *Sylvia's Lovers*, the heroine's silence is a denial of her sexuality, but whereas in each of those novels the plot turned upon a lie which confirmed that denial, *Cousin Phillis* turns on Paul's spoken recognition of Phillis's love. Vaguely conscious that his repetition of Holdsworth's speech can produce no possible social response from Phillis, Paul regrets his 'want of wisdom in having told "that thing" ' (p. 291), but when modern critics also see his speech as an 'error of judgment' (Keating, p. 28) they tacitly align themselves with the Victorian ideals of Phillis's father. Mr Holman's rage with Paul depends on his idea of girlhood as uniquely fragile. While he deals realistically with the little boys who spill the milk, on the basis that boys will be boys (p. 233), he sees Paul's speech to Phillis as having done irreversible harm. Like Elizabeth Gaskell's friend W.R. Greg, he believes that in women, 'desire is dormant, if not non-existent, till excited' (Greg 1850: 457), and that it is Paul who has ' "put such thoughts into the child's head ... to spoil her peaceful maidenhood

... raising hopes, exciting feelings ... it was more than wrong – it was wicked – to go and repeat that man's words" ' (C: 307–8). Paul, however:

> could not help remembering the pinafore, the childish garment which Phillis wore so long, as if her parents were unaware of her progress towards womanhood. Just in the same way the minister spoke and thought of her now, as a child, whose innocent peace I had spoiled by vain and foolish talk. I knew that the truth was different. (p. 307)

At the crux of the story, Phillis, for Paul's sake, defies the taboo and confirms her own sexuality to her father. Though ' "sick with shame" ' she speaks the necessary words, ' "I loved him, father!" ' (p. 308) and falls back, apparently 'dead' into a 'brain fever' (pp. 309–10). It may be 'Paul's error of judgment that precipitates Phillis's illness' (Keating, p. 28), but it is only an error in the context of contemporary ideology. By responding to Phillis's real emotion instead of her assumed silence, Paul widens the gap between Ceres and the Sleeping Beauty to the point of mental collapse, but he does not create the gap. And it is not simple disappointment but the shame of feeling unsolicited love which makes Phillis 'sick'. Like Thekla in Elizabeth Gaskell's story, *Six Weeks at Heppenheim* (1862), she might say, ' "my sorrow, which is also my reproach and my disgrace ... my shame ... is this: I have loved a man who has not loved me" ' (K7: 374).

Her recovery from acute illness does not free her from shame and silence; she 'lay for hour after hour quite silent on the great sofa' (C: 316) in that negative lassitude which was a kind of Victorian ideal (Ehrenreich and English 1979: 98–9), Ceres imprisoned in Sleeping Beauty's castle, unable to formulate any thought which did not relate to inadmissible goals. Margaret Ganz is indignant that it should be 'the good-natured scolding of an old servant woman' (Ganz 1969: 229) which delivers Phillis from this imprisonment, but it is Betty's perspective as a working woman which shows her the absurdity of treating a ' "woman" ' like a ' "baby" ' (C: 298). Betty is no prince and cannot rescue Phillis with a kiss, but she can suggest an alternative pattern of maturity. She is herself associated with the seasonal activities which made Hope Farm appear an idyll, and by urging Phillis to ' "do something for [her]self" ' (p. 316) she presents ' "the peace of the old days" ' as a state of purposeful activity, not suspended animation. Phillis's last words, ' "I can, and I will!" ' (p. 317) suggest a concept of maturity independent of a prince, and not therefore put out of bounds by shame.

Unlike Ruth, Phillis performs no sexual act, but her story raises some of the same questions about innocence and shame. The answers suggested by the earlier novel were inadequate because they were framed in the same biblical language which was the source of difficulty. In *Cousin Phillis* the Darwinian language of natural growth has replaced the concept of sin. There is, therefore, unconscious irony in Keating's description of *Cousin Phillis* as 'a tale of lost innocence'. While orthodox Victorians thought that innocence could be preserved inside a hedge of silence, *Cousin Phillis* shows 'that the truth was different' (p. 307). Phillis falls in love spontaneously, and the 'innocence' she loses is that of protracted childhood. In the context of Victorian ideology, this 'loss' cannot register as an unequivocal gain; the story cannot deny shame as a social fact. But *Cousin Phillis* does insist that women inevitably grow to maturity, and by diverting its focus from sexual attachment to self-sufficiency, from original sin to future development, it does evade the complacent pastoral melancholy which accepts female shame as a fact of nature.

Chapter Ten

Wives and Daughters (1865)

It is by the arts of *pleasing* only, that WOMEN can attain to
any degree of consequence or of power.
(The New Female Instructor: 1)

Can [these weak beings] be expected to govern a family
with judgment, or take care of the poor babes whom they
bring into the world?
(A Vindication of the Rights of Woman: 6)

Elizabeth Gaskell's last novel is a critical anomaly. While
it is 'generally felt to be her best' (Butler 1972: 278), 'one
of the great novels of any age' (Duthie 1980: xi), most
critics seem unable to account for its excellence except
'as a pleasant excursion... to the faraway world of her
childhood with Jane Austen as her travelling companion'
(Lansbury 1975: 182). Although Lerner notices that the
title 'announce[s] a theme' (*WD*: 16), he does not discuss
it, while Collins bluntly calls the title 'an irrelevance'
(Collins 1953: 60). Only Coral Lansbury and Patricia

Spacks see that the structure of families and the socialisation of girls is the central, and important, subject-matter of *Wives and Daughters*.

In 1862 Turgenev published *Fathers and Sons*, which became known to English *litterati* through the French translation. Turgenev had visited Manchester in 1859 and had friends, like the Nightingales, in common with Elizabeth Gaskell (Shapiro 1978: 126). If the title *Wives and Daughters* was intended as a reference to *Fathers and Sons*, the difference in formulation is significant. Turgenev's novel shows a radical, scientific son reacting against a feudal, authoritarian father. Elizabeth Gaskell, also dealing with parent-child relations, cannot simply transpose the pattern across gender boundaries, however, because mothers and daughters are defined primarily not by their relation to each other but by their relation to men. Whereas a vigorous son eventually assumes the authority of his father, a daughter is deflected into another subordinate role as wife, a role which also limits the power of mothers.

We have seen that in Elizabeth Gaskell's earlier novels, however 'public' the overt subject-matter, the story is deflected into personal relationships. Although this has been read as degeneration into romance or melodrama, the problem arises because it is impossible for Elizabeth Gaskell's female protagonists to speak and act as she thinks rational, humane people should without getting entangled in notions of feminine propriety. In the novels before *The Life of Charlotte Brontë* the problem seems unconscious, though we can trace it through disturbances of the text, inconsistencies, rhetoric and what Gillian Beer calls 'that oceanic richness . . . of symbol typical of Victorian prose' (G. Beer 1983: 14). *Wives and Daughters* for the first time makes central what had earlier been an unacknowledged problem: the education of daughters by wives to be wives.

The novel begins at the beginning, with 'the old rigmarole of childhood' (WD: 35), and the first two chapters are full of references to fairy tales. Like modern feminists, Elizabeth Gaskell recognised the force of these ritual stories told to children in forming expectations. Not only was she familiar with all the standard collections, but in her story *Curious if True* (1860; K7) she shows their living force by describing a castle full of fairy-tale characters transformed into Victorian social types.

Just as many fairy tales suggest rites of passage or initiation tests by which girls and boys become women and men, so *Wives and Daughters* begins with motherless Molly Gibson at the age of 12 (the conventional age for puberty), putting on new, festive clothes, leaving her father and home and entering the enclosed grounds of a house called The Towers, where she loses her god-mothers, falls asleep and is awakened by a lady with several names who will later become her stepmother. As 'A Novice Amongst the Great Folk' (Ch. 2), Molly is shown adult life at its most stately and hierarchical. Lord Cumnor, who frightens her by pretending to be Father Bear to her Goldilocks (WD: 53), is a mixture of fairy-tale grotesque and genuine feudal and patriarchal power, 'a cross between an archangel and a king' (p. 39).

The ritual phrases of these first chapters suggest that adults perceive female adolescence not as an active phase of growth but as a period of unconscious waiting, marked by allusion to 'the Sleeping Beauty, the Seven Sleepers, and any other famous sleepers' (p. 53). Molly's own father is no fairy-tale ogre; humorous and affectionate, he has given her 'excellent mothering' (Davidson and Broner 1980: 98). But he too conceives a sharp disjunction between the child and the woman, and instructs her governess not to 'teach Molly too much... I want to keep her a child' (*WD*: 65). Like Cousin Phillis, Molly thus appears to leap from being a baby 'in long-clothes' to having 'a lover' (p. 176), which defines her as nubile. Young Mr Coxe's 'passion' for Molly (p. 81) throws Mr Gibson into a panic because he conceives of her growth not as a natural process but as a knot in the thread of fate (p. 90), a 'Gordian knot' (p. 122). Like Sleeping Beauty's father, who tried to guard his daughter from the fairy's curse, the pricked finger, the ritual shedding of blood which signifies womanhood, Mr Gibson's one thought is that Molly must be guarded (p. 87), and since he is too busy as a country doctor to be always with her, he acquires Mrs Kirkpatrick as her stepmother.

If we take 'mothers' as the absent term in the title *Wives and Daughters*, it is significant that Molly acquires, not a mother but a stepmother. Modern feminists agree that patriarchal structures have driven a wedge between mothers and daughters, because the necessary social-isation of daughters into wives is perceived by the daughter as an outrage which could be perpetrated only by a 'false' or 'step-' mother. Chodorow describes how, as daughters grow up, they split their mother-image, often projecting the 'good', nurturing qualities on to the father and perceiving the 'bad' social control exercised by the mother as that of a stepmother (Chodorow 1978: 122–4). As a literary 'character', Mrs Kirkpatrick/Gibson is rightly regarded as a triumph, but most critics see her as no more than a 'neat satire' (Allott 1960: 29) of 'human deficiency' (McVeagh 1970a: 85; cf. Ganz 1969: 166). Only Patricia Spacks has fully understood that Mrs Gibson's 'imperfections' are not simply 'human' but specifically related to the ideology of the pleasing female.

Mrs Gibson's educational priorities match those of *The New Female Instructor*, the first six chapters of which deal with 'Dress and Fashion', 'Behaviour and Manners', 'Company', 'Conversation', 'Visiting and Amusements' and 'Employment of Time'. Her conversations with her own daughter, Cynthia, are almost all about dress, and when she gives a dinner-party, 'Cynthia and Molly looked their best, which was all the duty Mrs Gibson absolutely required of them' (*WD:* 306). Mary Wollstonecraft, lamenting the 'insipid' conversation of women 'whose time is spent in making caps, bonnets, and the whole mischief of trimmings', suggests that 'gardening, experimental philosophy, and literature, would afford them subjects to think of and matter for conversation, that in some degree would exercise their understandings' (*W:* (83). But Mrs Gibson calls Molly a ' "blue-stocking" ' when she reads Roger's books (*WD:* 307-8), and gardening makes her look ' "more like a delving Adam than a spinning Eve" ' (p. 373). Mrs Gibson herself has a technique of making 'indifferent trifles' assume 'infinite importance' (p. 358), and though Molly's 'never-ending feminine business' takes the shape of 'small duties' (p. 114), Spacks is right to contrast her 'relentless triviality of endeavour' with 'Roger Hamley's steady development toward a scientific career, or Mr Gibson's industry as a doctor' (Spacks 1976: 89). Molly is being taught to attain power not through knowledge or action but indirectly.

In order to 'attain... power', the 'pleasing' woman must know how to 'bend the haughty stubbornness of man' with 'an insinuating word' (*NFI:* 1-2); as Patmore approvingly puts it, 'To the sweet folly of the dove,/She joins the cunning of the snake' (*The Angel in the House* VIII, Prelude 1 [1862]). Mrs Gibson has been a governess, a curate's wife, a paid companion, a schoolmistress and a doctor's wife. In the paid situations, 'she must wear a cheerful face, or be dismissed' (Wollstonecraft [1787] 1972: 71). She therefore smiles pleasantly as she accedes to all requests (*WD:* 55) and makes speeches like 'soothing syrup' (p. 352), 'exactly the remarks which are expected from an agreeable listener' (p. 130). Her pliability, however, is self-interested; 'she must...be plastic herself if she would mould others' (Sandford 1831: 3), and although employment is a necessary stop-gap, her ultimate goal is marriage, which provides 'some one who would work while she sate at her elegant ease' (*WD:* 138). Lansbury calls her 'a slightly inefficient calculating machine' (Lansbury 1975: 206) and much of the comedy of the book arises from her rapid cost–benefit analyses of, for instance, an invitation (e.g. *WD:* 526, 666, 679).

Her calculation of Osborne Hamley's life-expectancy, which leads her to encourage Roger and Osborne alternately as suitors for Cynthia, is less amusing, though to her it seems quite laudable ' "to get Cynthia well married" ' (p. 429) and only ' "common sense" ' to choose the most prosperous brother (p. 428). Although the text is constructed so that we can 'see through' 'The Mother's Manoeuvre' (Ch. 35), it is important to realise that Mrs Gibson is not showing idiosyncratic villainy or caprice. 'Common sense itself is...rooted in a specific historical situation and...a particular social formation' (Belsey 1980: 3), so that Mrs Gibson justifies herself by an appeal to the 'unquestioned assumptions' (p. 4) of a whole society which thought that a woman who failed to marry had 'failed in business' (*Saturday Review* 8 [1859]: 576).

Though critics in general are amused by Mrs Gibson's bland hypocrisy, only feminists have seen that 'it is vain to expect virtue from women till they are in some degree independent of men....Whilst they are absolutely dependent on their husbands they will be cunning, mean, and selfish' (*W:* 154–5). Adrienne Rich sees a further 'danger run by all powerless people: that we forget we are lying, or that lying becomes a weapon we carry over into relationships with people who do not have power over us' (Rich 1980: 189). The very last paragraph of the (unfinished) novel is a wonderful exposure of how the 'art of pleasing' promotes habitual dissembling (*WD:* 705).

In that last scene, Mrs Gibson is irritated with Molly's refusal to learn her kind of selfish 'altruism'. But she is not the only source of Molly's education in womanhood; she is surrounded by role-models. Even the Miss Brownings grew out of a moral tale for children about a pair of pigeons called Pecksey and Flapsey (*Howitt's Journal* II [1847]: 284). Mrs Hamley conforms closely to the conduct-book model of the angel in the house, in whom 'weakness is an attraction, not a blemish' (Sandford 1831: 13), and self-sacrifice is Christlike (Johnson 1975: 25). She is 'gentle and sentimental; tender and good' (*WD:* 74) and having given up a great deal for her husband, sinks 'into the condition of a chronic invalid' (p. 73). Hers is a more sincere version of attaining power through the art of pleasing, but although she becomes 'the ruling spirit of the house' (p. 285), the novel suggests that her 'heated and scented' life (p. 76) is an unhealthy model for Molly. Where Mrs Sandford writes approvingly of the 'sedative' qualities of home duties (Sandford 1831: 169), *Wives and Daughters* is more critical. The drowsy stillness of Hamley Hall is compared with the ' "moated grange" ' (*WD:* 116) in Tennyson's 'Mariana' – a married version of Sleeping Beauty in her castle, perennially awaiting a relief which 'cometh not'.

Rather than any of these 'stepmothers', it is Molly's

father who offers a model which she is prepared to accept. His daily devotion to suffering people deeply affects her as a kind of altruism which is neither selfish nor sentimental (*WD:* 209). On the other hand, it is hardly acknowledged under a manner of brisk practicality and humour. Spacks sees this as an example of self-suppression common to both sexes in Victorian culture (Spacks 1976: 93), but the treatment of Thornton and Higgins in *North and South* defines obsessive refusal of emotion as characteristic of 'masculinity' (see above, Ch. 7), only indirectly imposed on women. Having decided that his marriage with Mrs Kirkpatrick is for Molly's 'good', for instance, Mr Gibson refuses to discuss it with her, and she is effectively silenced: 'she could not tell what words to use. She was afraid of saying anything, lest the passion of anger, dislike, indignation – whatever it was that was boiling up in her breast – should find vent in cries and screams, or worse, in raging words that could never be forgotten' (*WD:* 145). In spite of his rectitude and care, Mr Gibson thus emerges as only the most attractive of a long line of fallible fathers – John Barton, Parson Jenkyns, Mr Bradshaw, Mr Hale, Daniel Robson, Mr Holman – from whom their daughters must fight free.

It is at this juncture, in Chapter 10, that Roger Hamley is introduced as a significantly different sort of man. In all Elizabeth Gaskell's earlier novels, the nurturing impulses felt by men have been shown as repressed or distorted by the public languages of masculinity – impersonal, analytical, aggressive. But Roger's chosen discipline of natural history is presented as one in which there is no disjuncture between 'science' and personal relations. Roger is a keen observer, whose ' "eyes are always wandering about, and see twenty things where I [his father] only see one" ' (p. 105), and in Chapter 10 his pursuit of a rare plant brings him to Molly, who has hidden herself in the wood to vent her forbidden anguish (p. 148). Where Susan Griffin sees men and scientists as universal rapists of women and nature, Elizabeth Gaskell, a hundred years earlier, was able to present Roger as 'so great a lover of nature that, without any thought, but habitually, he always avoided treading unnecessarily on any plant; who knew what long-sought growth or insect might develop itself in that which now appeared but insignificant? (WD: 148). His attitude in fact conforms to all three qualities identified by Sara Ruddick as characteristic of 'maternal thinking'; rooted in care, it takes the form of constant and acute attention to detail, and expects change and growth (Ruddick 1980: 353, 357–8). It is consistent with such 'scientific' habits that Roger both pays attention to Molly's distress and longs 'to be of some little tender bit of comfort to her' (WD: 152), and that his scientific 'teaching' is expressed in 'maternal' terms: he 'cherished her first little morsel of curiosity, and nursed it into a . . . desire for further information' (p. 155). His moral prescription ' "to try to think more of others than of oneself" ' is offered in the same spirit, not as something appropriate for a woman, but what he himself has found ' "comfort" ' in (p. 152). His well-intentioned assumption of comparability be-tween them has a long-term effect in helping to release Molly from 'the intimidation of inequality' which she feels in relation to her father (Gilligan 1977: 507). Its immediate effect, however, is to trap her in a feminine role from which she must find her own release.

Molly is an ordinary girl, anxious to be undistin-guished, but her relatively unconventional, motherless girlhood, tutored by her clear-sighted, witty father, has made her relatively self-assertive and outspoken. In Chapter 3 she flies to the defence of her governess (WD:

67), and later she speaks her mind to both Lady Cumnor (p. 165) and Lady Harriet (p. 199). Likewise she resists Roger's prescription with some force: 'thinking more of others' happiness than of her own was very fine; but did it not mean giving up her very individuality, quenching all the warm love, the true desires, that made her herself?' (p. 169). When Roger says she will be happier in the end, she is vehement: ' "No, I shan't. . . . It will be very dull when I shall have killed myself, as it were, and live only in trying to do, and to be, as other people like" ' (p. 170). Here the image of feminine death, which has had a buried existence in the earlier novels, surfaces in its major signification: altruism is a threat to life.

The plain speaking fostered by her father's rationality, however, succumbs to his emotional silence. Where Roger's spoken advice allows reasoned objection, her father's silent evasion can only be met with silence. 'Mr Gibson did not want speech or words. He was not fond of expressions of feeling at any time' (p. 155). It is in this context that Molly comes to see Roger's prescription as the 'clue to goodness and peace' (p. 172) and embraces it as a 'new...larger system of duty' (p. 181) much as Maggie Tulliver embraces *The Imitation of Christ*. Roger has shifted Molly from Carol Gilligan's 'first stage' of youthful egoism into a 'second stage' of altruism which he assumes is his own (Gilligan 1977: 492). What neither of them recognises is that Roger, as a young man, has effortlessly assumed the 'third stage' in which 'obligation extends to include the self as well as others' (p. 506), so that he takes as a duty as well as a right his Cambridge education, freedom to travel, publish, court public recognition and reward. Molly, confined to 'relentless triviality', may make Roger her 'Mentor' (*WD:* 172), but she cannot, like Telemachus, share his route through life. The *Bildungsroman* which, for a male protagonist, charts the voyage out from family to social identity, becomes, for a woman, 'The Voyage In' (Abel *et al.* 1983). Slowly the death-in-life of the ' "Daughter at Home" ' (*L:* 72) descends upon her; 'was it goodness, or was it numbness...? Death seemed the only reality' (*WD:* 245).

Although Mr Gibson is a humane man in a nurturing profession, his refusal to articulate emotion is a version of the 'masculine lie' (see above, Ch. 7), which prevents humane emotion becoming part of the dominant ideology. Masculine silence promotes not only dutiful self-suppression but deviousness and evasion in women. As Molly becomes aware of her stepmother's 'webs... distortions of truth', she keeps silence from 'the desire of sparing her father any discord'; she worries 'whether this silence was right or wrong', but 'her father's example of silence... made her hold her tongue' (*WD:* 407). Marilyn Butler disparages *Wives and Daughters* for its conventional attitude to truth-telling: 'the parental injunction – Thou Shalt Not Lie – is... merely handed down... [not] examined and... qualified' (Butler 1972: 289–90). But Mr Gibson's tacit injunction is 'Thou Shalt Not Speak', and the novel does examine the relation between silence and lying. As refusal of emotion, silence serves the 'masculine lie'; as an adjunct of cunning, it serves the pleasing female. *Wives and Daughters* thus supports Elaine Showalter's contention that secrecy is 'the fundamental and enabling condition of middle-class life' (in Wohl 1978: 104), in which women of necessity lead 'duplicitous lives' in 'a house full of secret chambers'. The heroine of *Lady Audley's Secret* (1862), Showalter comments, is 'devious and perfidious not because she is a criminal and mad, but because she is a lady and sane' (in Wohl 1978: 113).

This paradox, potential in the silence Molly adopts to

please her father, is developed in Cynthia Kirkpatrick, the product of Mrs Gibson's education. Cynthia suffers both the neglect of a mother whose priority must be to please others, and the restrictions of surveillance, like the censorship of her letters from school, which baffle rational action and force her into lies, secrets and silence (*WD:* 522). Lacking both affection and practical security (p. 517), yet constrained by feminine propriety, Cynthia has no alternative but to adopt the arts of the pleasing female, developing 'the most exquisite power of adaptation to varying people' (p. 254). Lacking the healthy self-approval Molly derived from her father, Cynthia remains 'forever dependent on the image reflected back from other people's eyes' (Berke and Berke, in Davidson and Broner 1980: 106), and when the images conflict, she is thrown into a ' "mental fever" ', a 'brilliancy' like 'the glitter of the pieces of a broken mirror, which confuses and bewilders' (*WD:* 389).

Cynthia's problem is that although she excels in the art of pleasing, attracting multiple offers of marriage, she does not relish marriage. Although her success with Mr Preston makes her feel ' "a little queen" ', what makes her feel ' "like Cinderella when the clock was striking twelve" ' (p. 520) is not losing Prince Charming but having to marry him after the ball is over. In this situation, moreover, statements of dislike are counter-productive (p. 531). Preston, like Rousseau, regards resistance as part of 'the art of pleasing', rousing pleasurable desire in men (*W:* 54, n. 1). Baffled, Cynthia the virgin huntress seeks to displace one Prince Charming by another – Roger Hamley, Mr Coxe, Mr Henderson – devious and perfidious 'because she is a lady and sane'. Like another famous virgin, Effie Ruskin, whom Elizabeth Gaskell knew at school, Cynthia is 'just like somebody in the Arabian Nights, who was making up her list of 1000 lovers' (*L*: 195). The conduct-book writers saw 'the wish of being admired' as inborn in women (Sandford 1831: 64), but Wollstonecraft and Gaskell understand that it is induced: 'only taught to please, women are always on the watch to please, and with true heroic ardour endeavour to gain hearts' (*W*: 63).

The sad ironies of Wollstonecraft's words pervade *Wives and Daughters*, and the notion of being 'on the watch' has resonances which link apparently diverse themes. At its most positive, Sara Ruddick identifies 'attention' as 'an *intellectual* capacity connected even by definition with love' (Ruddick 1980: 358). Quoting Iris Murdoch, she goes on, ' "the task of attention goes on all the time and at apparently empty and everyday moments we are 'looking', making those little peering efforts of imagination which have such important cumulative results" ' (p. 358). It is the linking of knowledge with care, and the rooting of both in tiny, changing details, which Ruddick sees as characterising 'maternal thinking'. It is a mode of thought often dismissed as 'feminine intuition', which can seem illogically at odds with 'the facts'. When 'facts' seem to prove Molly guilty of impropriety with Mr Preston, for instance, the 'illogical' Miss Phoebe rehearses what she has 'seen' of Molly's patience and gentleness, and in 'tearful defiance of facts', refuses to ' "believe anything against her" ' (*WD*: 580-1). The point here is that Miss Phoebe's 'attention' to Molly's behaviour over a period of time has furnished her with alternative 'facts' which are real and valid, though less susceptible to legalistic 'proof'.

Ruddick's contention that such 'attention is an *intellectual* capacity' is an important challenge to the generally unexamined assumption of difference between nurturing/emotional/intuitive habits of mind and

scientific/intellectual/rational ones. Ruddick herself opposes 'maternal thinking' to the controlled, repeatable
experiments of science (Ruddick 1980: 353), just as
George Eliot prefers 'a picture of human life' to
'generalizations and statistics' ('The Natural History of
German Life', *Westminster Review*, July 1856: 54) and
Elizabeth Gaskell prefers 'actual personal contact' to
'mere institutions' (*NS*: 525). But the Victorian women,
who witnessed the transformation of natural history
from an 'amateur' activity (i.e. pursued out of love) to a
'science' (i.e. 'observed facts...brought under general
laws', *OED*), were in a better position to see that loving
attention to detail and its systematic classification are
not opposed mental qualities but different stages in an
ongoing process. What goes wrong with 'scientific
thinking' is that it forgets its origins; the 'general laws'
do not merely organise but displace the observed detail.
Moreover, since experience and education are required
to formulate 'general laws', these become the property
and distinguishing mark of the superior class and
gender, while women (and workers) are left with the
'observed detail'. While 'detail' may be a respectable
pursuit if it requires expeditions or laboratories, the
detail of everyday life is devalued and denied.

In *Wives and Daughters: An Everyday Story* Roger Hamley
demonstrates that there is no essential difference
between the 'attention' required for scientific knowledge and that which creates the 'intuitive' knowledge of
most women's daily life. In Chapter 10, for instance, he
examines two abnormal leaves of the ash-tree with the
same care with which he reads Molly's 'eloquent' look of
pain (p. 150), just as Molly 'knew her father's looks as
well as she knew her alphabet' (p. 214). Six years later
George Eliot deplores the fact that Dr Lydgate brings 'a
much more testing vision of details and relations into

[his] pathological study than he had ever thought it necessary to apply to the complexities of love and marriage' (*Middlemarch*, Ch. XVI). The professional-isation of 'natural history' led to its progressive separation from personal life and hence eventually to the real and potential horrors of, say, reproductive technology (cf. Arditti *et al.* 1984).

Whereas the natural sciences now form part of a general technocracy which aspires to the condition of mathematics, Elizabeth Gaskell wrote at a time when 'natural history' was still close to everyday life and hence promised a wholeness of view in which detail was not submerged in 'general laws'. For her, the threatening masculine science was political economy, the dominant language of Victorian industrial capitalism (see above, Ch. 7). The fact that women feel threatened not by 'scientific thinking' itself but by the historical separation of the dominant language from personal life, is demonstrated by Roger Hamley's brother Osborne, who, as a classical scholar and man of letters, represents the exclusive language whereby men separated them-selves from womanly trivia in pre-industrial society. Writing in 1796, Elizabeth Gaskell's father saw this traditional education as the same sort of threat to an integrated consciousness as feminists now see in a masculine 'science'. 'A mere classical scholar is not, by his knowledge, connected with the world. Whereas every branch of natural science is to him, acquainted with it, a link, which connects him with his fellow-men' (Steven-son 1796: 28). Thus Osborne's poeticism leads him to ignore details in favour of generalisations about 'love' and 'beauty'. He doesn't ' "exactly know when dog-roses are in flower!" ' (*WD*: 351) and cannot 'read', from his father's restless movements, his willingness to be reconciled (p. 479).

Women, on the other hand, do not have an 'integrated consciousness' by virtue of their sex; 'maternal thinking' requires a link between attention and care. Mrs Gibson, the pleasing female, is impatient with 'details' (p. 209) and acts on shifting and spurious 'principles', (p. 212). She is 'an unperceptive person, except where her own interests were dependent upon another person's humour' (p. 214). Her 'attention' to other people is factitious, based not on 'love' but 'self-love'. Cynthia is essentially similar. When her mind wanders from a scientific discussion, she pleads, ' "It is quite true!...I was not attending" ', giving the phrase a schoolroom flavour of compulsion. Molly, in contrast, 'was trying to understand with all her might', because she cares for Roger (p. 307). Normally, Cynthia perfectly counterfeits the 'attention' which seems to be linked with care. At the Miss Brownings', her 'sweet eyes were fixed upon [Roger's] face with a look of great interest in all he was saying' (p. 278), which she later dismisses with a yawn (p. 281). It is this 'counterfeit' attention, which falsely indicates the depth of care, which makes Molly 'chafe' at Cynthia's engagement to Roger. Though she could have 'cut off her right hand' to please him, Molly is tortured by perceiving him as the victim of 'plots' in which 'Cynthia [is] the conscious if passive bait' (p. 390).

Thus, though families are made of people who are 'on the watch' and 'attention' is ideally linked with 'care', creating a body of knowledge which connects people with each other, the link is repeatedly broken by the 'secrecy' of family life. Mr Gibson's 'keen, observant eyes' identify love only as 'an unknown illness' (p. 698). Mrs Gibson's observations only serve her 'manoeuvres' (Ch. 35). Osborne's exacted promise of silence is a 'blank wall' which 'block[s] up the way' for Molly's sympathy (p. 248), and Cynthia's 'dead wall' of mystery marks a limit to her professions of love (p. 461). Mrs Gibson's 'care' of Molly takes the form of 'a most wearying supervision' (p. 506). Even Roger's love for Cynthia is a 'blindness' in which he is 'willingly... entrapped' (p. 390). No wonder that Molly's 'sun was all shrouded over with grey mist' (p. 456). It seems that she can only wait, like the Sleeping Beauty, for rescue.

The surprising turn to this 'voyage in', however, is that Molly is rescued not by an external agent but by her own initiative in rescuing Cynthia from Mr Preston. While Roger quests for fame and fortune in foreign lands, Molly finds an alternative testing-ground among the secret chambers of family life, an enterprising version of the Nonconformist injunction to 'Do the duty that lies nearest to thee' (Carlyle, quoted in *L* 72). Rather than playing the role of the fairy-tale daughter, who enters womanhood in a state of sleep, Molly usurps the part of the younger son, who passes tests, fights duels, rescues damsels. Armed with the courageous truth-telling habits of her youth, she is, in Elizabeth Gaskell's approving phrase, a 'law unto herself' (*L* 101). Typically, however, Victorian girls were 'left untested' (Vicinus 1972: ix), and although Molly's blameless weapons are straight looks (*WD*: 509), a straight path (p. 525) and straight talk (p. 531), she cannot take initiative without creating scandal. If Portia lived in Victorian England, Anna Jameson said, she would not be 'a gracious, happy, beloved and loving creature', but 'a victim, immolated in fire to that multitudinous Moloch termed Opinion' (quoted in Rubenius 1950: 44). Nevertheless, although Molly is ostracised, her semi-public act of rescue does not sink her in shame as does Margaret Hale's, and the chapter-headings – 'Molly Gibson to the Rescue' (Ch. 44) and 'Molly Gibson Finds a Champion' (Ch. 49) – suggest a tongue-in-cheek relish entirely lacking in the earlier

novel. The positive quality derives from female friendship. There is wry satisfaction in Cynthia/Cinderella
being rescued not by but from a Prince Charming, and
by a Molly, and Molly's own chivalrous 'champion' is
Lady Harriet, who enlists Miss Phoebe as ' "Sancho
Panza" ' to her ' "Don Quixote" ' – ' "you and I against the
world, in defence of a distressed damsel" ' (p. 581).

This female solidarity is the more striking in a fairy-
tale framework since fairy tales, in their function as 'text
books' of 'the myths of sexuality under patriarchy'
(Duncker 1984: 3), normally endorse enmity between
women, who become rivals for the father's approval
(p. 7). The most distressing aspect of Cynthia's affair
with Mr Preston is that she and her mother are rivals
(*WD*: 518), and her again *Wives and Daughters* reads like a
demonstration of Wollstonecraft:

> supposing... that a being only taught to please must still
> find her happiness in pleasing; what an example of folly...
> will she be to her innocent daughters! The mother will be
> lost in the coquette, and, instead of making friends with her
> daughters, view them with eyes askance, for they are
> rivals – rivals more cruel than any other, because they
> invite a comparison, and drive her from the throne of
> beauty, who has never thought of a seat on the bench of
> reason. (*W*: 55)

Thus Mrs Kirkpatrick keeps Cynthia away from her
wedding because 'she had felt how disagreeable it would
be to have her young daughter flashing out her beauty
by the side of the faded bride' (*WD*: 156), and in the last
pages of the novel she is still appealing for confirmation
that she is 'the fairest of them all' (p. 703).

In Elizabeth Gaskell's rewriting of fairy tale, however,
Molly not only acts as champion to her sister but also
challenges the word of the father. In her interview with

Mr Gibson she takes moral control: ' "I don't think it was wrong.... You must trust me.... Perhaps I've been foolish; but what I did, I did of my own self.... Cynthia must not be accused.... You must not vex or hurt Cynthia" ' (pp. 568–72). This is the voice of a woman who, by being 'a law unto herself', is able to protect others without using the 'arts of pleasing'. Although Molly's status and prospects are not changed by this episode, it is nevertheless crucial to her psychological escape from the 'secret chambers' of family life. Carol Gilligan's study of modern women considering abortion shows that their sense of being trapped by or in control of their lives depends less on external circumstances than on their conception of themselves in relation to others. Women in the 'third' or most ethically mature stage are characterised by a 'willingness to express and take responsibility for judgment', indicating 'an equation of worth between self and other' (Gilligan 1977: 507).

The sense of self-worth expressed in Molly's new relation to her father is further developed in the affair of Osborne's marriage. Again involved against her will in a family secret, it is she who decides when to keep silent and when to speak, and who takes charge of the shattered Hamley household, controlling the servants and caring for Aimée and the Squire (WD: 634–5). The chapter in which 'Molly Gibson's worth is Discovered' (Ch. 54) is curiously disparaged by critics. Lerner passes over the hard slog of domestic management which has taxed Molly's health and says that she suffers 'one of those low-spirited declines into which Victorian heroines drop at low moments of the plot' (WD: 8), while Marilyn Butler finds *Wives and Daughters* inferior to Maria Edgeworth's *Helen* because 'Molly collapses not because she has suffered too much but because she has done too much, a very different thing' (Butler 1972: 287).

Certainly, but why inferior? As in *North and South*, it is salutary to be shown that 'thinking of others' is not just a question of 'sympathis[ing] in their feelings' (Sandford 1831: 2) but of exhausting work. More importantly, Molly's progress towards autonomy is to be measured precisely in terms of her change from 'suffering' to 'doing', which even within a domestic environment, makes a woman 'of far more importance ... than she usually thinks she is' (Mrs Beeton, quoted in Auerbach 1978: 35; see above, Ch. 2 (1)). The main effect of what Molly 'does', however, is to dispel secrecy.

Both secrets which Molly is left to disentangle – Cynthia's and Osborne's – involve sexual alliances which cannot be socially acknowledged, and the novel forcibly establishes the sense of Victorian marriage as a public institution and a strongly conservative force. The great families like the Cumnors and the Hamleys maintain their status through long descent and careful alliance. Squire Hamley is obsessively concerned that Osborne, as 'eldest son' should make an appropriate marriage, warning off the Gibson family and uncertain whether even Lord Hollingford's daughters would be suitable (*WD*: 88, 107, 112, 115, 413). He is both snobbish and chauvinistic, hating the French with ignorant vehemence (pp. 344, 624). Mrs Gibson has the social climber's contradictory concept of marriage as a route to social advancement for herself, and an excluding mechanism for everyone else. Her 'Mother's Manoeuvre' is even more callous than Squire Hamley's prohibitions of love, in spite of her 'sweet, false tone' (p. 359).

For the upholders of ancient lineage and exclusive alliance, however, the text holds a lurking irony: its plot depends on the challenge made to human hierarchies by the anarchic processes of sexual selection identified by Darwin. Mr and Mrs Gibson (pp. 81, 178, 703), Cynthia,

Roger (p. 391), Mr Preston (p. 492) and Mr Coxe (p. 448) all fall in love more than once and sometimes with most unsuitable objects (p. 659). Mr Preston persists in his 'tigerish' love for Cynthia against her wishes and his self-interest. The free play of sexual charm creates havoc in the Cynthia/Preston[Kirkpatrick triangle. Osborne Hamley marries a French nursery-maid, ineligible in every way except that she is 'Aimée' – loved. By defining this process as a general law rather than shockingly anomalous, 'Darwinian theory... brought into question the privileged "purity" of the "great family"' (G. Beer 1983: 63, cf. 117). In *Wives and Daughters* Darwinian sexual anarchy takes the form of subversive family secrets – Cynthia's engagement, Osborne's marriage – raising 'the same dreads as fairy-tale... miscegeny – the frog in the bed' (G. Beer 1983: 9). Whereas fairy tales are essentially conservative, however, showing Cinderella or the frog prince as miraculous exceptions to a rule (Duncker 1984: 5), Darwinian transformations constitute a pervasive and relentless rule, capable of undermining the notions of 'pure blood' and 'ancient lineage' which preserve families in their traditional form. If secrecy is the 'enabling condition of middle-class life' (Showalter, in Wohl 1978: 104), then someone like Molly who is prepared to reveal secrets for humane reasons acquires potentially transforming power, and it is Molly who prevents the Hamleys from succumbing to 'The Doom of the Griffiths' (see above, Ch. 3 (Coda)). There is considerable irony in the fact that after Mrs Hamley's and Osborne's deaths, almost every aspect of the Hamley household lies in the control of a girl who was not judged fit to marry into the family. A more basic irony, however, is that Squire Hamley, the epitome of autocratic will and patriarchal pride, should have one son – Osborne – who weakly evades the patri-

lineal imperative to 'marry well', and another – Roger –
who builds a flourishing career on the very evolutionary
theory which subverts the unnatural *stasis* of old families
(e.g. *WD: 72*).

Roger Hamley was directly modelled on Elizabeth
Gaskell's cousin, Charles Darwin (*L 550*), and her
enthusiastic acceptance in *Wives and Daughters* of evolutionary theory both as a scientific truth and as a mode
of social progress was more characteristic of Unitarian
thought than the panic response of *Sylvia's Lovers*. 'Alone
among the Christian sects the Unitarians rejoiced as
they saw the plan of nature being unfolded without
recourse to marvel or mystery' (Lansbury 1975: 194).
Far from being a dreamy retreat into rural nostalgia,
therefore, *Wives and Daughters* reflects the most advanced
preoccupations of its time. The struggle to develop science
rather than the classics as the staple of education, to
which Elizabeth Gaskell's father had contributed in 1796
(Stevenson, *Remarks on the Very Inferior Utility of Classical
Learning*), reached its height in the 1860s (Costic 1982:
51). William Gaskell was 'absorbed in the new scientific
studies' (Gérin 1976: 52), and in 1861 arranged a
meeting of the British Association for the Advancement
of Science (*L 485*). Given this history, and in the
immediate aftermath of *The Origin of Species*, it is
extraordinary that the evolutionary matrix for social
change in *Wives and Daughters* has been ignored by
influential critics such as John Lucas, who sneers at 'Mrs
Gaskell' for her inability to trascend class sympathies
and recognise Preston, rather than Roger Hamley, as the
'rising man' (Lucas 1977: 11). Lucas, taking class conflict
as the only mechanism of change, selects Chapter 30, a
scene between men in a work situation, and assumes
that Roger and his father align unproblematically in
class terms against Preston. Yet the relationship

between the three men is equally determined by Roger's deference to paternal authority (see Ch. 27) and by the sexual rivalry between Roger and Preston (see Chs. 28, 29). Lucas argues that Elizabeth Gaskell's class animus 'betrays' her 'into absurdity' when she describes Preston as having 'an animal's instinctive jealousy and combativeness against all popular young men' (quoted in Lucas 1977: 11). But she is likely to have had in mind not class conflict but Darwin's conception of 'Sexual Selection' which 'depends, not on a struggle for existence in relation to other organic beings or to external conditions, but on a struggle between the individuals of one sex, generally the males, for the possession of the other sex' (*The Origin of Species*, Everyman edn, 1928: 87). The choice of marriage partners in relation to class boundaries is an important factor in social change, and the authority of a father can be as strong a force for reaction as that of a landlord. Lucas sees Elizabeth Gaskell as 'fudging' the issue (Lucas 1977: 1) when she is perceiving complexity.

Preston is in any case an unattractive 'new man'. Whereas the social operations of science are genuinely 'levelling' (*WD:* 68, 180), Preston merely climbs the existing class structure (p. 188). And in personal relationships he functions at an animal level ' "tigerish, with his beautiful striped skin and relentless heart" ' (p. 523), and his sinister insistence that he will ' "make" ' Cynthia love him ' "when we are married" ' (pp. 512, 530). In contrast, Roger relies on the distinctly human functions of reason and speech.

In spite of a certain relish for the 'levelling' effects of sexuality in *Wives and Daughters*, Elizabeth Gaskell was in no doubt that uninhibited sexuality was a danger rather than a freedom, 'an arbitrary passion, [which] will reign...by its own authority, without deigning to reason' (*W:* 129). But the earlier novels have shown that sexuality remains unsusceptible to reason partly because contemporary codes of 'innocence' and 'propriety' prevent its conscious articulation. The concept of virtue as unreasoned submission to rules is both a source of distress and a barrier to ethical maturity for women. *Wives and Daughters* still does not attempt the articulation of desire, but it does enlarge the area accessible to consciousness, and hence to rational control, by insisting that relationships between the sexes involve the same connection between attention and care which, ideally, governs those between parents and children, brothers, sisters and friends. As we have seen, all these essentially caring relationships are corrupted by the contagious secrecy surrounding Victorian sexuality. Molly, as a genuine 'innocent', can 'express and take responsibility for judgment' (Gilligan 1977: 507) in these areas not because she can speak of sexuality itself but because, on the contrary, she lacks the heightened sexual sensitivity which underlies both coquettish manoeuvrings and frigid propriety. Her ethical judgements are based, therefore, not on concepts of rule-breaking or of 'sin' but on the general 'obligation to exercise care and avoid hurt' which Gilligan sees as characteristic of women's 'Different Voice' (Gilligan 1977: 486, 491–2, 507).

The only examples in *Wives and Daughters* of the acute physical dis-ease which accompanies sexual repression in *Ruth* and *North and South* occur when Molly is parted from Roger. News of his expedition causes 'a buzzing in her ears' (*WD:* 408), and his proposal to Cynthia produces a response which, with its buried quotation from one of Wordsworth's Lucy poems, recalls both Phillis's similar silent suffering (see Ch. 9, above) and Molly's own prediction that she will ' "kill herself" ' with altruism (*WD:* 170); 'her brain seemed in too great a whirl to comprehend anything but that she was being carried on in earth's diurnal course, with rocks, and stones, and trees, with as little volition on her part as if she were dead' (pp. 417-8). In each of these cases, however, the distress is caused not simply by sexual deprivation but by the inability of the 'brain' to 'comprehend' and hence to 'express and take responsibility for judgment' (Gilligan 1977: 507).

In the earlier novels the problem is beyond rational remedy because shame prohibits full consciousness. Molly, however, is not 'ashamed' of a relationship which she defines to herself as friendship, and her lack of sexual awareness is enabling rather than the reverse because she can freely articulate this 'innocent' willingness to care. Even after Roger's engagement, 'she had courage to speak, and she spoke the truth as she believed it, though not the real actual truth. "I do care for him: I think you have won the love of a prince among men" ' (WD: 422). She can, moreover, get some ethical purchase on her situation by applying the same criteria of care which would operate in other relationships. Her conscious renunciation of Roger, made in the terms of the real mother in Solomon's test – ' "give her the living child, and in no wise slay it" ' (p. 460) – is a sad but responsible position. What puts her brain 'in a whirl' is the suspicion that her self-sacrifice will not 'avoid hurt' for Roger (Gilligan 1977: 492), since Cynthia's fascination conceals a lack of the care which it seems to promise. In Roger's absence, Cynthia receives his letters 'with a kind of carelessness,... while Molly sat at her feet, so to speak, looking up with eyes as wistful as a dog's waiting for crumbs (WD: 458-9). Although Molly seems to be released from this thraldom by mere authorial *fiat*, the engagement crumbles from within. Cynthia is incapable of sustaining a relationship of care, and her 'short, hurried letters' only give Roger 'pain' (p. 699).

The courtship ritual whereby a man 'pays his attentions' to a woman, who may invite, welcome or refuse them, is itself based on the assumption that 'attention' promises 'care', and though anarchic and unspeakable sexuality may not be under our control, our attention should be. As Molly puts it, ' "all sorts of thoughts cross one's mind – it depends whether one gives them harbour and encouragement" ' (p. 696). When Mrs Gibson learns of Osborne's secret marriage, she is indignant; ' "Only think! If he had paid either of you any particular attention, and you had fallen in love with him! Why, he might have broken your heart" ' (p. 618). But Osborne, as a (relatively) responsible person, refrains from paying attentions to women whom he cannot 'care for'. Mr Preston, on the other hand, pays 'compliments' which mean nothing, while his 'attentions' to Cynthia have as their object his gratification, not hers. Women, though conventionally passive, could welcome or refuse such 'attentions'; Molly discourages Mr Coxe by withdrawing 'her open friendliness of manner', while Cynthia 'drew him to her' by 'her look of intent interest' (p. 448). By exercising no control over her 'attention', Cynthia raises expectations of care which she cannot fulfil. Mr Preston's refusal to accept her withdrawal of attention, on the other hand, claims care where none is offered. Bestowing or withholding attention is thus, even within Victorian conventions, a means of controlling sexuality and bringing sexual relations into conformity with other relationships involving 'care and attention'. When Molly protests against women marrying ' "unless we love someone very dearly indeed" ', Mrs Gibson sees her ' "tirade" ' as ' "really rather indelicate, I must say" ' (p. 650). Molly's insistence on love, however, exposes Cynthia's 'pleasing' and Mr Preston's 'gallantry' as lies, promising care they do not intend to give.

Over-rigorous propriety, on the other hand, requires a 'lying' refusal of attention even where care exists. Molly, brought up as a companion to her father, regulates her friendship with Roger by habits of care and attention in which gender is irrelevant. Her dealings with Mr Preston are also so entirely formulated by the matter in hand that she 'was as unconscious that he was a young man, and she a young woman, as if she had been a pure angel of heaven' (p. 533). But before her final visit to Roger at Hamley Hall (Ch. 59), Mrs Goodenough's hints force on her a shameful consciousness which spoils 'the simplicity of their intercourse' and prevents her from treating Roger with more than 'common politeness' (p. 683). Her 'constraint' (p. 685) and 'reserve' (p. 686) prevent her even from seeking his advice; 'she believed that he could have helped her more than anyone to understand how she ought to behave... if only he himself had not lain at the very core and centre of all her perplexity and dismay' (p. 691). Thus 'propriety' shuts her out from moral advice, just as 'surveillance' prevents Cynthia from disentangling herself from Mr Preston (p. 522). Roger in turn is 'perplexed and pained' by a withdrawal of attention which he interprets as an absence of care (p. 697).

The painstaking detail of the conversations in *Wives and Daughters* supports a general plea for the power of speech in establishing a more open and rational intercourse between the sexes, in which the arts of pleasing shall not masquerade as love, and propriety shall not exclude care. It is disappointing that Molly allows Roger to take the initiative in their final *éclaircissement*, which leaves her 'red as a rose' (p. 691).

Nevertheless his simple question and her direct reply suggest a potential for communication and trust which is a significant advance on the secrets and silence of their parents, and in this context the novel's evasion of explicitly sexual consciousness is less of a fault than it might appear. Molly's 'innocence' is not the dangerous ignorance of Ruth, unable to distinguish Bellingham's 'attentions' from love, and her ability to affirm friendship for a man saves her from the crippling shame of Margaret Hale and Cousin Phillis. When the author makes a motherly little joke at her expense, as she waves goodbye to Roger and thinks 'how sweet is friendship!' (p. 702), her innocence seems an endearing aspect of her youth, but the refusal of sexual shame is also the basis of womanly strength.

The book's unfinished state underlines 'questions about the "happy ending" ' for Molly and Roger; in particular, 'what is she to do with him, how is she to live?' (Spacks 1976: 94–5). Although Molly is interested enough in Roger's work to impress Lord Hollingford with her intelligence and information (*WD*: 339), there is no question of her pursuing a career. Yet modern readers hardly feel satisfied with a novel which leaves its heroine in the state of stifling self-sacrifice implied by Victorian wife- and motherhood. The introduction of Aimée and her child suggests, however, that the novel which started with a *critique* of Molly's various mother-substitutes was to end with some comment on alternative modes of motherhood. Even as a dutiful daughter Molly has achieved a kind of self-affirmation through truth-telling amid the secret chambers of family life; Aimée's widowhood and her escape from the Squire's immediate influence (p. 698), with Roger's care and respect for the independent lives of other people, suggest that Aimée and Molly as young mothers would be less constrained than their elders by their roles as wives. Like Mary Wollstonecraft, Elizabeth Gaskell recognised that 'making women better mothers' (Banks and Banks 1964: 17) is not a question of intensifying devotion but, on the contrary, of strengthening women's autonomy to the point where they can 'govern a family with judgment' and 'take care' of their children (W: 6) in a different sense from any of Molly's 'stepmothers'. Mrs Hamley, the most devoted of these maternal models, would have got little sympathy from Wollstonecraft: 'women of sensibility are the most unfit for this task.... [It] requires the sober steady eye of reason' (p. 75). Wollstonecraft's heroines, by contrast, are 'poor women [who] maintain their children by the sweat of their brow, and keep together families that the vices of the fathers would have scattered abroad...who have had few advantages of education, and yet have acted heroically' (p. 84).

Significantly, Mrs Hamley's place at the Hall is taken, after her death, by a woman who, despite her frail, pretty appearance, is not unlike Wollstonecraft's model. Aimée has worked as a nursery-maid and is in fact 'a very capable person' (WD: 626). Left destitute not by Osborne's vices but by his improvidence, she travels with prompt efficiency to Hamley Hall with her son, a 'sturdy, gallant, healthy little fellow, whose every limb, and square inch of clothing, showed the tender and thrifty care that had been taken of him' (p. 629). She ' "has been well trained in the management of children" ' (p. 697) and her loving and practical motherhood makes an irony of Osborne's attempts to romanticise her as 'Lucy' in his sonnets (p. 300), and of the Squire's complaint that Osborne did not marry ' "as befitted one of an old stock" ' (p. 688). Whereas in much 'wishful Victorian literature... heroines... prove... to have aristocratic blood' (G. Beer 1983: 63), this heroine, installed in an ancient family, is a genuine working woman with practical skills.

Molly herself is repeatedly linked with servants. During her first visit to the Towers she is mistaken for a French nursery-maid (*WD*: 53); moreover, aristocratic life makes her feel like an extinguished candle (p. 58), and she vehemently wishes ' "never [to] be a lord or a lady" ' (p. 59). She has been brought up by a 'strong, alert' servant called Betty (p. 66), and Mrs Goodenough thinks that, with a name like Molly, ' "she might as well be a scullery-maid at oncest" ' (p. 552). When Mrs Goodenough describes how Molly met Mr Preston alone, ' "just as if she was my Betty, or your Jenny" ', she means to cast doubt on her propriety, but given Elizabeth Gaskell's general respect for working women, we can equally read it as showing that Molly has assumed some of the 'fighting spirit' of such unprotected women; her stories are full of loving and capable servant-women, from Nancy in *The Moorland Cottage* to Betty in *Cousin Phillis* (see above, Ch. 3 (1)). Aimée's rise from rags to riches seems like a fairy-tale structure, but the fact that Molly's story is a less extreme version of the same Cinderella theme allows us to see it as a Darwinian transformation rather than a unique metamorphosis; an example of an evolutionary process which, with sexual selection as its rather alarming dynamic, and human care and attention as its control, lessens, without dramatic upheaval, the distance between classes and genders. Admittedly the more disturbing aspects of sexual determinism only became apparent, in Darwin's *Descent of Man* (1871), after Elizabeth Gaskell's death, and her meliorism may appear merely Utopian to post-Freudian feminists. Nevertheless, her emphasis on observation, reason and speech as gradual modes of social progress may still be the only way of avoiding, on the one hand, a tragic biological determinism and, on the other, a defiance of patriarchy which incorporates patriarchy's own aggressive modes.

When Molly pays her second visit to The Towers (Chs. 57–8), she finds that her habits of observation and truth-telling enable her to analyse, rather than accepting, the fairy-tale structures of power. The lords and ladies are just another family (p. 671), and the archangel/king is less important than her friends Lady Harriet and Roger, who are her 'peers' in attention to truth and care for people. But when she tries to recount this reorientated tale to her godmothers, she is 'conscious of her stepmother's critical listening' and has 'to tell it all with a mental squint' (p. 680). The title of *Wives and Daughters*, with its sidelong look at *Fathers and Sons*, announces the lifelong 'squint' of daughters who must please stepmothers whose looking-glass 'speaks with the King's voice' (Gilbert and Gubar 1979: 46). But as Mrs Gibson in the last sentence falls into a fireside doze, we are reminded that her final manoeuvre has been thwarted, as 'Molly stood out' for the family being seen 'as they really were' (*WD*: 705).

Conclusion

She had courage to speak, and she spoke the truth as she believed it.

(WD: 422)

Between *Mary Barton* and *Wives and Daughters* Elizabeth Gaskell has shifted from public to private themes, from fatherhood to motherhood, and from a self-conscious use of Romantic or biblical allusion to the language of family life. The change has been interpreted as her giving up the struggle for social reform and becoming, in late middle-age, gracefully 'feminine' and conformist. What this study has shown, on the contrary, is that each of the earlier novels 'tripped' on the unfocused 'woman question' which in *Wives and Daughters* becomes the acknowledged subject of debate.

The problematic status of *Wives and Daughters* as a 'great' novel with nothing to account for its 'greatness' – no dramatic events, 'major' themes, revolutionary conclusions – is related to the minuteness of its effects, dictated by the small scale of women's daily lives but also by the theories of Realism. Because Elizabeth Gaskell was not a theorist like George Eliot, the philosophical arguments for Realism have not been related to her work; as Laurence Lerner ingenuously puts it, 'if Mrs Gaskell can't be let off [literary theory], who can? (WD: 23). Yet by the time George Eliot was writing in favour of close observation of detail as the basis for a 'wise social policy' (*Westminster Review*, July 1856: 72), Elizabeth Gaskell was already established as a major writer in this mode and was herself suspected of having written *Adam Bede* (L 431), with its 'Realist manifesto' (Ch. XVII). She, in turn, admired George Eliot, and is likely to have read her essay, 'The Natural History of German Life' (*Westminster Review*, July 1856), advocating the methods of natural history as a way of understanding human societies. *Wives and Daughters*, with its explicit reference to natural history, reveals Elizabeth Gaskell as a classic Realist, confident in the ability of free individuals to make rational choices in a knowable world.

For the modern academic reader, Realism is suspect precisely because it has become the dominant mode of fiction, part of our culture's dominant discourse of liberal, rational humanism. Post-structuralists see Realist texts as, *par excellence*, purveyors of ideology, offering the illusion of unified, autonomous individuals and obscuring the construction of the speaking subject in language (Belsey 1980: 67–84). The deconstructive critic does not interpret, thus endorsing, the text's illusory coherence, but works on its contradictions to expose as ideology what it offers as reality. Thus where an 'interpretation' of *Ruth* would accept the novel's evaluative terminology as 'given' and hence 'real', my reading points to the contradiction between Ruth's bodily experience and the language available to speak about it, revealing female sexuality as the 'hidden' subject-matter which ideology renders 'unspeakable' and hence 'unreal'.

If my reading of *Wives and Daughters* seems by contrast to collude with its ideological language, it is because the novel's overt Realist project, to observe, analyse, and offer a 'wise ... policy' about women's lives, is itself the 'meaning' which has been 'hidden' by previous 'interpretations', which have focused on class, science, humour – anything but wives and daughters. When orthodox criticism 'overlooks' meanings that are announced in the title, we may suspect that those meanings are themselves ideologically 'unspeakable', and this encourages me to argue that when a woman writer usurps the 'authority' of the Realist stance to investigate the lives of women, her text has a subversive rather than confirmatory relation to the dominant mode. Elizabeth Gaskell's claim to participate in the 'liberal humanist discourse of freedom, self-determination and rationality' (Belsey 1980: 65) from which women were conventionally excluded, makes her assumption of the dominant paradoxically also a challenge to it, a challenge which has not yet lost its force.

I would not wish to endorse this rational discourse to the extent of denying its contradiction with the text's conventional assumptions about 'woman's place'. But feminist criticism seeks not just to understand, but to change the world, and must sometimes compromise with deconstructive rigour in order to introduce ethical or political value-judgements. In challenging a false 'coherence', deconstruction may perversely establish its own multivalent pluralism as a new infallibility, inhibiting any reading of less than immaculate scepticism. If, however, we 'lock up our... thoughts till infallibility has set its seal upon them... priestcraft and intolerance would... strangle... free opinion' (W. Gaskell 1862: 5). Deconstruction performs a mobilising social role in so far as it breaks open texts which present themselves as 'the truth', making possible the production of new meanings. For speakers who are oppressed precisely by being told that their different view of the world is 'unreal', however, the claim to know and speak the truth, though ultimately illusory, is politically vital.

Realism, with its emphasis on detail and gradualness, and its assumption that knowledge is a route to self-determination and power, can speak in practical ways to modern women who experience politics as an intimate, daily and material practice, yet doubt that their knowledge is 'real' because it lacks the authority of a general truth and takes instead the form of a constant, shifting negotiation of detail, aimed not at 'principled' changes, but simply 'that resolution in which no one is hurt' (Gilligan 1977: 515). Both George Eliot and Elizabeth Gaskell, in their adoption of Realism, emphasise their preference for detail over abstraction, and gradual over revolutionary change, because such knowledge and mode of change allows for the play of 'moral sentiments' (*Westminster Review*, July 1856: 54).

Marxist critics protest at this 'displacement' of history into ethics as 'a mystification inherent in the very forms of realist fiction, which by casting objective social relations into interpersonal terms, constantly hold open the possibility of reducing the one to the other' (Eagleton 1978: 121). I have argued that such a 'reduction' invalidates the ending of *Mary Barton*, for instance. Feminists who believe that the personal is political should beware, however, of assuming that private acts are unhistorical; for women, politics begins with challenging the 'private' acts which forbid them a public voice. Politics, moreover, is not unrelated to ethics; attempts to change the world are normally justified in ethical terms – equality, free enterprise, the right to work – and women have so far made headway in public politics by invoking just such 'principles of justice' (Gilligan 1977: 484) – the right to vote, the right to choose. It is usual, however, to distinguish these 'abstract ethical conception[s]' from the more contextual ethics of women in the home. As Gilligan says, 'the very traits that have traditionally defined the "goodness" of women, their care for and sensitivity to the needs of others, are those which mark them as deficient in moral development', allowing an 'infusion of feeling into their judgement' (p. 484). More and more feminists, however, are beginning to argue that caring is the authentic voice of women, and that women's 'insistence on relationship reveals not a failed adulthood, but the desire for a different one' (Abel, in Abel *et al.* 1983: 10). Changing the world is a question of bringing politics into conformity with ethics, and women speak of ethics 'In a Different Voice' (Gilligan 1977). 'Faced with a hypothetical moral dilemma, women often ask for more information.... [We] need to talk to the participants, to see their eyes and facial expressions, to receive what they are feeling. Moral decisions are... made in real situations; they are qualitatively different from the solution of geometry problems' (Noddings 1984: 2–3).

The vital unsolved problem now facing the women's movement is to give this authentic women's voice political force without adopting the masculine language of rights and principles which leads to self-righteous belligerence. It is a problem energetically tackled in, for instance, Keohane, Rosaldo and Gelpi's *Feminist Theory* (1982). In the meantime, the women Realists of the past can help give validity to women's knowledge of 'real situations' and our wish for resolutions in which 'no one is hurt'. If we deal with these writers by labelling them 'progressive' or 'conservative' according to the outcome of their plots or their fictional technique, we may miss the genuine challenge of their 'different voice'. In Elizabeth Gaskell's novels, 'caring for others' requires not subservience and conformity but courage and independence. Her heroines may not differ in institutional terms from other dutiful daughters, wives and mothers, but they have achieved that sense of self-worth which is the prerequisite for political action; they 'express and take responsibility for judgment' (Gilligan 1977: 507). She may use current, common modes of analysis and speech, but she insists that women share in the creation of values. From Esther the outcast prostitute, who for Mary's sake speaks as a 'fighting mother', to Molly the cherished daughter, who for Cynthia's sake questions the word of the father, Elizabeth Gaskell's women refuse to 'suffer and be still'. Moved by human need, they claim a human voice to 'bear witness to the truth'.

Alphabetical List of References

Abel, Elizabeth (ed.). 1982. *Writing and Sexual Difference* (Harvester: Brighton; University of Chicago Press: Chicago, 1980).

—— *et al.* (eds.). 1983. *The Voyage In: Fictions of Female Development* (University Press of New England: Hanover, NH).

Allott, Miriam. 1960. *Elizabeth Gaskell* (Longman: Burnt Mill).

Anderson, Nancy. 1982. 'No Angel in the House: The Psychological Effects of Maternal Death', *Psychohistory Review* 11, 20–46.

Arditti, Rita, *et al.* (eds.). 1984. *Test-Tube Women: What Future for Motherhood?* (Pandora Press, Routledge & Kegan Paul: London).

Auerbach, Nina. 1978. *Communities of Women* (Harvard University Press: Cambridge, Mass., and London).

Banks, J.A. and Banks, Olive. 1964. *Feminism and Family Planning in Victorian England* (Liverpool University Press: Liverpool).

Bardwick, Judith M. 1971. *Pscyhology of Women: A Study of Bio-Cultural Conflicts* (Harper & Row: New York and London).

Barker, Francis *et al.* (eds.). 1978. *The Sociology of Literature: 1848* (University of Essex).

Barrett, Michèle (ed.). 1979. *Virginia Woolf: Women and Writing* (The Women's Press: London).

Basch, Françoise. 1974. *Relative Creatures: Victorian Women in Society and the Novel 1837–67*, trans. Anthony Rudolph (Allen Lane: London).

Beer, Gillian. 1983. *Darwin's Plots: Evolutionary Narrative in Darwin, George Eliot and Nineteenth-Century Fiction* (Routledge & Kegan Paul: London and Boston).

Beer, Patricia. 1974. *Reader, I Married Him: A Study of the Women Characters of Jane Austen, Charlotte Brontë, Elizabeth Gaskell and George Eliot* (Macmillan: London).

Belsey, Catherine. 1980. *Critical Practice* (Methuen: London and New York).

Bergmann, Helena. 1979. *Between Obedience and Freedom: Women's Role in the Mid-Nineteenth Century Industrial Novel* (Acta Universitatis Gothenburgensis: Gothenburg, Sweden).

Bodichon, Barbara Leigh Smith. 1854. *A Brief Summary in Plain Language of the Most Important Laws Concerning Women* (no publisher cited).

Bremer, Fredrika. 1843. *The Home: or, Family Cares and Family Joys*, trans. Mary Howitt, 2 vols., 2nd edn (Longman & Co.: London).

Butler, Marilyn. 1972. 'The Uniqueness of Cynthia Kirkpatrick: Elizabeth Gaskell's *Wives and Daughters* and Maria Edgeworth's *Helen*', *Review of English Studies*, NS 23, 278–90.

Calder, Jenni. 1976. *Women and Marriage in Victorian Fiction* (Thames & Hudson: London).

Cazamian, Louis. 1973. *The Social Novel in England 1830–1850*, trans. Martin Fido (Routledge & Kegan Paul: London and Boston; first published 1903).

Cecil, Lord David. 1934. *Early Victorian Novelists: Essays in Revaluation* (Constable: London).

Chapple, J.A.V. 1967. ' "North and South": A Reassessment', *Essays in Criticism* 17, 461–72.

—— 1980. *Elizabeth Gaskell: A Portrait in Letters* (Manchester University Press: Manchester).

Chesler, Phyllis. 1974. *Women and Madness* (Allen Lane: London).

Chodorow, Nancy. 1978. *The Reproduction of Mothering* (University of California Press: Berkeley, Los Angeles and London).

Collins, H.P. 1953. 'The Naked Sensibility: Elizabeth Gaskell', *Essays in Criticism* 3(1), 60–72.

Costic, Linda Seidel. 1982. 'Elizabeth Gaskell and the

Alphabetical List of References

Question of Liberal Education', *University of Hartford Studies in Literature* 14(2), 50–60.

Craik, W.A. 1975. *Elizabeth Gaskell and the Provincial Novel* (Methuen: London).

Crick, B. 1976. 'Mrs Gaskell's *Ruth*: A Reconsideration', *Mosaic* 9(2), 85–104.

Cudden, J.A. 1979. *A Dictionary of Literary Terms* (Penguin: Harmondsworth).

Daly, Mary. 1979. *Gyn/Ecology: The Metaethics of Radical Feminism* (Women's Press: London; Beacon Press: Boston, 1978).

David, Deidre. 1981. *Fictions of Resolution in Three Victorian Novels: North and South, Our Mutual Friend, Daniel Deronda* (Macmillan: London).

Davidson, Cathy N. and Broner, E.M. (eds.). 1980. *The Lost Tradition: Mothers and Daughters in Literature* (Frederick Ungar: New York).

Davis, Angela. 1982. *Women, Race and Class* (Women's Press: London; Random House: New York, 1981).

Delphy, Christine. 1977. *The Main Enemy: A Materialist Analysis of Women's Oppression* (Women's Research and Resources Centre Publications: London).

Dinnerstein, Dorothy. 1976. *The Rocking of the Cradle and the Ruling of the World* (Souvenir Press: London); published in New York by Harper & Row as *The Mermaid and the Minotaur: Sexual Arrangements and Human Malaise.*

Dodsworth, Martin. 1963. 'Women Without Men at Cranford', *Essays in Criticism* 13, 132–45.

Duncker, Patricia. 1984. 'Re-Imagining the Fairy Tales: Angela Carter's Bloody Chambers', *Literature and History* 10(1), 3–14.

Duthie, Enid L. 1980. *The Themes of Elizabeth Gaskell* (Macmillan: London).

Eagleton, Terry. 1976. ' "Sylvia's Lovers" and Legality', *Essays in Criticism* 26(1), 17–27.

—— 1978. *Criticism and Ideology: A Study in Marxist Literary Theory* (Verso: London; New Left Books: London, 1976).

—— 1983. *Literary Theory: An Introduction* (Basil Blackwell: Oxford).

Easson, Angus. 1979. *Elizabeth Gaskell* (Routledge & Kegan Paul: London, Boston and Henley).

Ehrenreich, Barbara and English, Deidre. 1979. *For Her Own Good: 150 Years of the Experts' Advice to Women* (Pluto Press:

London; Anchor Press/Doubleday, New York, 1978).

Ellis, Mrs [Sarah, née Stickney]. 1839. *The Women of England; their social duties, and domestic habits* (Fisher, Son & Co.: London).

—— 1845. *The Daughters of England: Their Position in Society, Character and Responsibilities* (Fisher, Son & Co: London and Paris).

Ellmann, Mary. 1979. *Thinking About Women* (Virago, London; Harcourt, Brace and World: New York, 1968).

Empson, William. 1935. *Some Versions of Pastoral* (Chatto & Windus: London).

Fetter, F.W. 1960. 'The economic articles in *Blackwood's Edinburgh Magazine*, and their authors, 1817–1853', *Scottish Journal of Political Economy* 7, 85–107.

[Froude, J.A.] 1847. *Shadows of the Clouds*, by Zeta (John Ollivier: London).

—— 1852. 'The Oxford Commission', *Westminster Review* 58 (NS 2), 317–48.

Fryckstedt, Monica Correa. 1982. *Elizabeth Gaskell's "Mary Barton" and "Ruth": a challenge to Christian England* (Almquist and Wiksell: Stockholm).

Furbank, P.N. 1973. 'Mendacity in Mrs Gaskell', *Encounter* 40, 51–5.

Ganz, Margaret. 1969. *Elizabeth Gaskell: the Artist in Conflict* (Twayne Publishers: New York).

Gaskell, William. 1862. 'Unitarian Christians Called to Bear Witness to the Truth...' (Edward T. Whitfield: London).

Gérin, Winifred. 1976. *Elizabeth Gaskell: A Biography* (Oxford University Press: Oxford and New York).

Gilbert, Sandra and Gubar, Susan. 1979. *The Madwoman in the Attic: The Woman Writer and the Nineteenth-Century Literary Imagination* (Yale University Press: New Haven, Conn., and London).

Gilligan, Carol. 1977. 'In a Different Voice: Women's Conceptions of Self and Morality', *Harvard Educational Review* 47, 481–517.

Gorham, Deborah. 1982. *The Victorian Girl and the Feminine Ideal* (Croom Helm: London and Canberra).

Gornick, Vivian and Moran, Barbara K. (eds.). 1971. *Women in Sexist Society: Studies in Power and Powerlessness* (Mentor: New York).

[Greg, W.R.] 1850. 'Prostitution', *Westminster Review* 53, 448–560.

Alphabetical List of References

Griffin, Susan. 1984. *Woman and Nature: The Roaring Inside Her* (Woman's Press: London).

Grubb, Gerald G. 1943. 'Dickens' Editorial Methods', *Studies in Philology* 40, 79–100.

Guettel, Charnie. 1974. *Marxism and Feminism* (The Women's Press: Toronto).

Holt, Raymond V. 1938. *The Unitarian Contribution to Social Progress in England* (George Allen & Unwin: London).

Homans, Margaret. 1980. *Women Writers and Poetic Identity: Dorothy Wordsworth, Emily Brontë and Emily Dickinson* (Princeton University Press: Princeton, NJ).

Hopkins, Annette B. 1931. 'Liberalism in the Social Teachings of Mrs Gaskell', *Social Service Review* (Chicago) 5, 57–73.

—— 1952. *Elizabeth Gaskell: Her Life and Work* (John Lehmann: London).

Howitt, William. 1840. *Howitt's Visits to Remarkable Places* (Longham, Brown, Green, Longmans & Roberts: London).

Howitt, W. and Howitt, M. 1847–8. *Howitt's Journal of Literature and Popular Progress* (Lovett: London).

Jackson, Rosemary. 1981. *Fantasy: The Literature of Subversion* (Methuen: London and New York).

Jacobus, Mary. 1979. *Women Writing and Writing About Women* (Croom Helm: London; Harper & Row: New York).

Johnson, Wendell Stacey. 1975. *Sex and Marriage in Victorian Poetry* (Cornell University Press: Ithaca, NY).

Kaplan, Cora. 1976. 'Language and Gender', in *Papers on Patriarchy* (Women's Publishing Collective: London).

Keohane, Nannerl O., Rosaldo, Michelle Z., and Gelpi, Barbara C. (eds.). 1982. *Feminist Theory: A Critique of Ideology* (Harvester Press: Brighton).

Kettle, Arnold. 1958. 'The Early Victorian Social-Problem Novel', in *From Dickens to Hardy*, ed. Boris Ford (Penguin: Harmondsworth).

Kristeva, Julia. 1977. *About Chinese Women*, trans. Anita Barrows (Marion Boyars: London).

Lansbury, Coral. 1975. *Elizabeth Gaskell: The Novel of Social Crisis* (Paul Elek: London).

Lehmann, Rosamond. 1948. Introduction to *Wives and Daughters*, by Elizabeth Gaskell (Lehmann: London).

Lucas, John. 1966. 'Mrs Gaskell and Brotherhood', in *Tradition and tolerance in nineteenth-century fiction*, ed. David Howard *et al.* (Routledge & Kegan Paul, London).

—— 1977. *The Literature of Change: Studies in the Nineteenth-Century Provincial Novel* (Harvester: Brighton; Harper & Row: New York).

McKibben, Robert C. 1960. 'The Image of the Book in *Wuthering Heights*', *Nineteenth-Century Fiction* 15(2), 159–69.

McVeagh, John. 1970a. *Elizabeth Gaskell* (Routledge & Kegan Paul: London).

—— 1970b. 'The Making of "Sylvia's Lovers" ', *Modern Language Review* 65, 272–81.

Macherey, Pierre. 1978. *A Theory of Literary Production*, trans. Geoffrey Wall (Routledge & Kegan Paul: London and Boston).

Marks, Elaine and de Courtivron, Isabella (eds.). 1982. *New French Feminisms* (Harvester: Brighton).

Miller, Nancy K. 1981. 'Emphasis Added: Plots and Plausibilities in Women's Fiction', *Publications of the Modern Language Association of America* 96(1), 36–48.

Mitchell, Juliet and Rose, Jacqueline (eds.). 1982. *Feminine Sexuality: Jacques Lacan and the Ecole Freudienne* (Macmillan: London).

Moers, Ellen. 1978. *Literary Women* (Women's Press: London).

Newton, Judith and Rosenfelt, Deborah (eds.). 1985. *Feminist Criticism and Social Change* (Methuen: New York and London).

Noddings, Nel. 1984. *Caring: A Feminine Approach to Ethics and Moral Education* (California University Press: Berkeley, Los Angeles and London).

Norton, Caroline. 1854. *English Laws for Women in the Nineteenth Century* (printed by J. Wertheimer & Co., London).

O'Brien, Mary. 1981. *The Politics of Reproduction* (Routledge & Kegan Paul: Boston, London and Henley).

Plath, Sylvia. 1965. *Ariel* (Faber & Faber: London).

Pollard, Arthur. 1965. *Mrs Gaskell, Novelist and Biographer* (Manchester University Press: Manchester).

Rance, Nicholas. 1975. *The Historical Novel and Popular Politics in Nineteenth-century England* (Vision Press: London).

Reiss, Erna. 1934. *Rights and Duties of Englishwomen: A Study in Law and Public Opinion* (Sherratt & Hughes, Manchester).

Rich, Adrienne. 1977. *Of Woman Born: Womanhood as Experience and Institution* (Virago: London).

—— 1980. *On Lies, Secrets and Silence: Selected Prose 1966–1978* (Virago: London; W. W. Norton: New York, 1979).

Rubenius, Aina. 1950. *The Woman Question in Mrs Gaskell's Life*

Alphabetical List of References

and Works (A.-B. Lundequistka Bokhandeln: Upsala; Harvard University Press: Cambridge, Mass.)

Rubinstein, Marc A. 1976. ' "My Accursed Origin": The Search for the Mother in *Frankenstein', Studies in Romanticism* 15, 165–94.

Ruddick, Sara. 1980. 'Maternal Thinking', *Feminist Studies* 6 (2), 342–67.

Sandford, Mrs John [Elizabeth]. 1831. *Woman, in her Social and Domestic Character* (Longman, Rees, Orme, Brown & Green: London).

Selig, Robert I. 1977. *Elizabeth Gaskell: A Reference Guide* (G.K. Hall: Boston).

Shapiro, Leonard. 1978. *Turgenev: His Life and Times* (Oxford University Press: Oxford and New York).

Shelley, Mary. 1985. *Frankenstein*, ed. Maurice Hindle (Penguin: Harmondsworth; first published 1818).

Showalter, Elaine. 1975. 'Literary Criticism', *Signs* 1, 435–60.

—— 1978. *A Literature of Their Own* (Virago: London; Princeton University Press: Princeton NJ, 1977).

—— 1984. 'Looking Forward: American Feminists, Victorian Sages', *The Victorian Newsletter* 65, 6–9.

Smith-Rosenberg, Carroll. 1975. 'The Female World of Love and Ritual: Relations between Women in Nineteenth-Century America', *Signs* 1(1), 1–30.

Spacks, Patricia Meyer. 1976. *The Female Imagination: A literary and psychologial investigation of women's writing* (Allen & Unwin: London; first published in the United States).

Spender, Dale. 1980. *Man Made Language* (Routledge & Kegan Paul: London, Boston and Henley).

—— (ed.). 1983. *Feminist Theorists* (Women's Press: London).

Stevenson, William. 1796. *Remarks on the Very Inferior Utility of Classical Learning* (no publisher cited, Manchester).

—— 1824–5. 'The Political Economist', *Blackwood's Edinburgh Magazine* 15(88), 522–31; 15(89), 643–55; 16(90), 34–45; 16(91), 202–14, 17(97), 207–20.

Stone, Donald D. 1980. *The Romantic Impulse in Victorian Fiction* (Harvard University Press, Cambridge, Mass., and London).

Strachey, Ray. 1978. *The Cause* (Virago: London; first published 1928).

Stubbs, Patricia. 1979. *Women and Fiction: Feminism and the Novel 1880–1920* (The Harvester Press, Sussex).

Tarratt, Margaret. 1968. *'Cranford* and "the Strict Code of

Gentility" ', *Essays in Criticism* 18 (11), 152–63.

Tillotson, Kathleen. 1956. *Novels of the Eighteen-Forties* (Oxford University Press: Oxford and New York).

Tomalin, Claire. 1974. *The Life and Death of Mary Wollstonecraft* (Weidenfeld & Nicolson: London).

Trudgill, Eric. 1976. *Madonnas and Magdalens: The Origins and Development of Victorian Sexual Attitudes* (Heinemann: London).

U[pham], C[harles] W. 1831. *Lectures on Witchcraft: Comprising a history of The Delusion in Salem in 1692* (Carter & Hendee: Boston).

Vicinus, Martha. 1972. *Suffer and Be Still: Women in the Victorian Age* (Indiana University Press: Bloomington and London).

Weeks, Jeffrey: 1981. *Sex, Politics and Society* (Longman: London and New York).

Welch, Jeffrey. 1977. *Elizabeth Gaskell: An Annotated Bibliography 1929-75* (Garland Publishing: New York and London).

Wheeler, Michael D. 1974. 'The Writer as Reader in *Mary Barton', Durham University Journal* 67 (NS 36), 92–102.

—— 1976. 'The Sinner as Heroine: A Study of Mrs Gaskell's *Ruth* and the Bible', *Durham University Journal* 68 (NS 37), 148–61.

Williams, Raymond. 1958. *Culture and Society 1780-1950* (Chatto & Windus, London; Columbia University Press: New York).

Wohl, Anthony (ed.). 1978. *The Victorian Family: Structure and Stresses* (Croom Helm: London).

Wolfe, Patricia A. 1968. 'Structure and Movement in *Cranford', Nineteenth-Century Fiction* 23 (2), 161–76.

Wollstonecraft, Mary. 1972. *Thoughts on the Education of Daughters* (Augustus M. Kelly: Clifton, NJ; first published 1787).

—— 1976. *Mary, a Fiction and The Wrongs of Woman*, ed. Gary Kelly (Oxford University Press: London and New York; *Mary, a Fiction* first published 1788 and *The Wrongs of Woman* first published 1798).

Woolf, Virginia. 1977. *Three Guineas* (Penguin: Harmondsworth; first published 1938).

Wordsworth, William. 1963. *The Lyrical Ballads*, ed. R.L. Brett and A.R. Jones (Methuen: London; first published 1798).

Wright, Edgar. 1965. *Mrs Gaskell: The Basis for Reassessment* (Oxford University Press: London and New York).

Zaretsky, Eli. 1976. *Capitalism, the Family and Personal Life* (Pluto Press: London; first published in *Socialist Revolution* (Calif.), January–June, 1973).

Selected Bibliography

Elizabeth Gaskell

For editions, see References and Abbreviations (pp. 13-15). There are two bibliographies:

Selig, Robert L., *Elizabeth Gaskell: A Reference Guide* (G.K. Hall: Boston, 1977).
Welch, Jeffrey, *Elizabeth Gaskell: An Annotated Bibliography 1929-75* (Garland Publishing: New York and London, 1977).

The most useful biographical and critical works are:

Chapple, J.A.V., *Elizabeth Gaskell: A portrait in letters* (Manchester University Press: Manchester, 1980).
Gérin, Winifred, *Elizabeth Gaskell: A Biography* (Oxford University Press: Oxford and New York, 1980).
Lansbury, Coral, *Elizabeth Gaskell: The Novel of Social Crisis* (Paul Elek: London, 1975).
Rubenius, Aina, *The Woman Question in Mrs Gaskell's Life and Works* (A.-B. Lundequista Bokhandeln: Uppsala, 1950).

Victorian Women and Women Writers

Basch, Françoise, *Relative Creatures: Victorian Women in Society and the Novel 1837–67* (Allen Lane: London, 1974).

Gorham, Deborah, *The Victorian Girl and the Feminine Ideal* (Croom Helm: London, 1982).

Moers, Ellen, *Literary Women* (Women's Press: London, 1978).

Showalter, Elaine, *A Literature of Their Own* (Princeton University Press: Princeton, NJ, 1977; Virago: London, 1978).

Vicinus, Martha (ed.), *Suffer and Be Still: Women in the Victorian Age* (Indiana University Press: Bloomington and London, 1972).

Zaretsky, Eli, *Capitalism, the Family and Personal Life* (Pluto Press: London, 1976).

Feminist Theory and Literary Criticism

Abel, Elizabeth (ed.), *Writing and Sexual Difference* (Harvester Press: Brighton, 1982).

Belsey, Catherine, *Critical Practice* (Methuen: London and New York, 1980).

Chodorow, Nancy, *The Reproduction of Mothering* (University of California Press: Berkeley, Los Angeles and London, 1978).

Dinnerstein, Dorothy, *The Rocking of the Cradle and the Ruling of the World* (Souvenir Press: London 1976); published in New York by Harper & Row as *The Mermaid and the Minotaur; Sexual Arrangements and Human Malaise*.

Eagleton, Terry, *Literary Theory: An Introduction* (Basil Blackwell: Oxford, 1983).

Gilbert, Sandra, and Gubar, Susan, *The Madwoman in the Attic: The Woman Writer and the Nineteenth-Century Literary Imagination* (Yale University Press: New Haven, Conn., and London, 1979).

Gilligan, Carol, *In a Different Voice: Psychological Theory and Women's Development* (Harvard University Press: Cambridge, Mass. and London, 1982).

Jacobus, Mary, *Women Writing and Writing About Women* (Croom Helm: London; Harper & Row, New York, 1979).

Keohane, Nannerl O., Rosaldo, Michelle Z. and Gelpi,

Selected Bibliography

Barbara C. (eds.), *Feminist Theory: A Critique of Ideology* (Harvester Press: Brighton, 1982).

O'Brien, Mary, 1981. *The Politics of Reproduction* (Routledge & Kegan Paul: Boston, London and Henley).

Spender, Dale, *Man Made Language* (Routledge & Kegan Paul: London, Boston and Henley, 1980).

Index

218